I0762721

TO

FROM

DATE

BIBLE PROMISES

DaySpring
LIVE YOUR FAITH

Bible Promises for Women

Second Edition, June 2024

Published by:

21154 Highway 16 East
Siloam Springs, AR 72761
dayspring.com

Cover Design by: Becca Barnett

Printed in China
Prime: U2295
ISBN: 979-8-88602-721-1

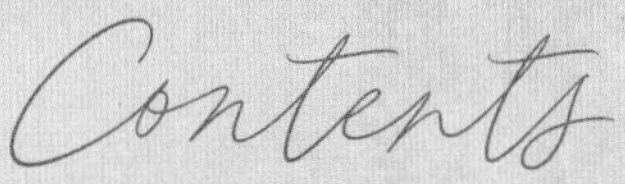

Introduction

The Bible is a book like no other. It is a gift from the Creator, a guidebook for life here on earth and a roadmap for life eternal. And it's a book of promises.

When God makes a promise, He keeps it. No exceptions. So the verses in this text are not hypotheticals; they're certainties. They apply to every generation, including yours, and they apply to every human being, including you.

Are you worried? Discouraged? Afraid? Trust the promises that God has made to you. Do you have a difficult task ahead? Ask your heavenly Father for courage. Do you have too many responsibilities and too little time to do them? Ask God to help you prioritize your day and your life. Whatever your circumstance, whatever your need, God is sufficient. No challenges are too big for Him, not even yours.

This book contains timeless promises and timely insights from notable women. The ideas on these pages are intended to remind you that the Lord is steadfast. Through the gift of grace, He offers eternal love and eternal life. It's a promise that you can depend on, now and forever.

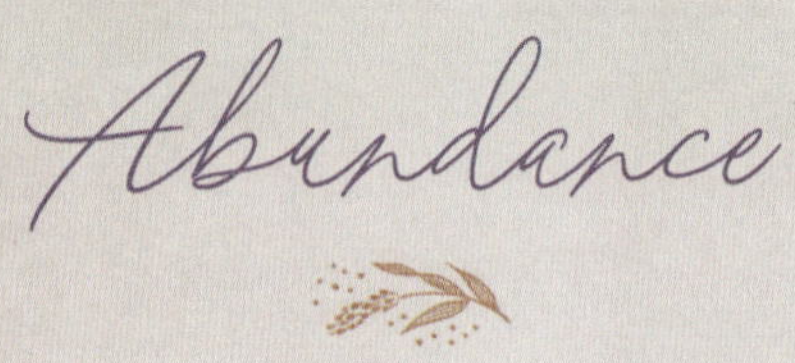

"I have come that they may have life,
and that they may have it more abundantly."
JOHN 10:10 NKJV

God's abundance is available to each of us. He offers His blessings, but He doesn't force them upon us. To receive them, we must trust His promises and follow, as closely as we can, in the footsteps of His Son. But the world tempts us to do otherwise.

Everywhere you turn, someone or something is vying for your attention, trying to convince you that peace and happiness are commodities that can be purchased for the right price. But, buyer beware. Genuine peace and spiritual abundance are not for sale at any price. Real abundance is never obtained through worldly possessions. It results from your relationship with God.

Do you seek the abundant life that Jesus promises in John 10:10? Then turn your life and your heart over to Him. When you do, you'll receive the love, the peace, and the abundance that can only come from the touch of the Master's hand.

If you want purpose

and meaning and satisfaction

and fulfillment and peace

and hope and joy

and abundant life

that lasts forever,

look to Jesus.

ANNE GRAHAM LOTZ

GOD'S PROMISES ABOUT ABUNDANCE

"Until now you have asked for nothing
in My name. Ask and you will receive,
that your joy may be complete."

JOHN 16:24 CSB

*And God is able to make all grace abound
to you, so that always having all sufficiency
in everything, you may have an
abundance for every good deed.*

II CORINTHIANS 9:8 NASB1995

Success, success to you,
and success to those who help you,
for your God will help you.

I CHRONICLES 12:18 NIV

*My cup runs over. Surely goodness and mercy
shall follow me all the days of my life; and I will
dwell in the house of the LORD forever.*

PSALM 23:5–6 NKJV

May the LORD bless you and protect you;
may the LORD make His face shine
on you and be gracious to you;

NUMBERS 6:24–25 CSB

Acceptance

Should we accept only good things from
the hand of God and never anything bad?

JOB 2:10 NLT

All of us encounter situations and circumstances that we wish we could change but can't. Sometimes the problems are simply too big for us to solve. Sometimes the things we regret happened long ago, and no matter how many times we replay the events in our mind, the past remains unchanged. And sometimes we're swept up by life-altering events that we simply cannot control.

Reinhold Niebuhr penned a simple verse that has come to be known as the Serenity Prayer. It begins with a simple yet profound request: "God, grant me the serenity to accept the things I cannot change." Niebuhr's words are far easier to recite than they are to live by. Why? Because most of us want life to unfold in accordance with our own wishes and timetables. But sometimes God has other plans.

If you've encountered unfortunate circumstances that are beyond your power to control, accept those circumstances. And trust God. When you do, you can be comforted in the knowledge that your Creator is good, that His love endures forever, and that He understands His plans perfectly, even when you do not.

Acceptance says,

"True, this is my situation

at the moment.

I'll look unblinkingly

at the reality of it.

But I'll also open

my hands to accept

willingly whatever

a loving Father sends."

CATHERINE MARSHALL

GOD'S PROMISES ABOUT ACCEPTANCE

Everything God made is good,
and nothing should be refused
if it is accepted with thanks.

I TIMOTHY 4:4 NCV

He is the Lord, and He will do what's right.

I SAMUEL 3:18 CEV

Trust in the Lord with all your heart
and lean not on your own understanding.

PROVERBS 3:5 NIV

For the Lord is good.
His unfailing love continues forever,
and His faithfulness continues
to each generation.

PSALM 100:5 NLT

For now we see in a mirror, dimly,
but then face to face. Now I know in part,
but then I shall know just as I also am known.

I CORINTHIANS 13:12 NKJV

Accepting Christ

"For God so loved the world, that He gave
His only begotten Son, that whosoever believeth in Him
should not perish, but have everlasting life."

JOHN 3:16 KJV

Jesus came to this world in order that each of us might live abundantly and eternally. He came so that our joy might be complete here on earth and, more importantly, in heaven. Christ loved us so much that He endured unspeakable pain on the cross so that we might be with Him throughout eternity.

How will you respond to Christ's sacrifice? Will you give Him your heart, your mind, and your soul? And will you accept the gift of eternal life, a gift that cost Him so much but can be yours for the asking? It's the most important decision you'll ever make. And if you choose wisely, it's a decision that you'll never regret.

When we end up in a situation where we have been rejected, there is an acceptance in Christ of a new place He is going to take us. It is like nothing we have ever experienced. You are accepted in Christ, never rejected by Him.

BETH MOORE

GOD'S PROMISES ABOUT ACCEPTING CHRIST

And this is the testimony: God has given us eternal life, and this life is in His Son. The one who has the Son has life. The one who does not have the Son of God does not have life.

I JOHN 5:11–12 CSB

For the wages of sin is death, but the gift of God is eternal life in Christ Jesus our Lord.

ROMANS 6:23 NIV

The Spirit of God, who raised Jesus from the dead, lives in you. And just as God raised Christ from the dead, He will give life to your mortal bodies by this same Spirit living within you.

ROMANS 8:11 NLT

Therefore we were buried with Him by baptism into death, in order that, just as Christ was raised from the dead by the glory of the Father, so we too may walk in newness of life.

ROMANS 6:4 CSB

"I am the good shepherd. The good shepherd lays down His life for the sheep."

JOHN 10:11 NIV

We are hard-pressed on every side, yet not crushed;
we are perplexed, but not in despair.
II CORINTHIANS 4:8 NKJV

Tough times. Disappointments. Hardship. Pain. These experiences are the inevitable cost that each of us must pay for being human. From time to time we all encounter adversity. Thankfully, we need never encounter it alone. God is always with us.

When we are troubled, God stands ready and willing to protect us. Our responsibility, of course, is to ask Him for protection. When we call upon Him in prayer, He will answer—in His own time and in His own way.

If you find yourself enduring difficult circumstances, remember that God remains in His heaven. If you become discouraged with the direction of your day or your life, turn your thoughts and prayers to Him. He is a God of possibility, not negativity. He will guide you through your difficulties and beyond them. And then, with a renewed spirit of optimism and hope, you can thank the Giver for gifts that are simply too numerous to count.

God will make obstacles serve His purpose.

LETTIE COWMAN

GOD'S PROMISES ABOUT ADVERSITY

I called to the LORD in my distress;
I called to my God.
From His temple He heard my voice.

II SAMUEL 22:7 CSB

The LORD is my rock, my fortress, and my deliverer, my God, my rock where I seek refuge. My shield, the horn of my salvation, my stronghold, my refuge, and my Savior.

II SAMUEL 22:2–3 CSB

God blesses those who patiently endure testing and temptation. Afterward they will receive the crown of life that God has promised to those who love Him.

JAMES 1:12 NLT

*He heals the brokenhearted
and bandages their wounds.*

PSALM 147:3 CSB

The LORD is my shepherd; I shall not want.

PSALM 23:1 KJV

Angels

Do not neglect to show hospitality to strangers,
for by this some have entertained angels without knowing it.

HEBREWS 13:2 NASB1995

The Bible promises that God sends angels to protect His children. He did so in biblical times, and nothing has changed since then. Our beloved heavenly Father still sends emissaries to guide and protect His own.

Perhaps you don't spend much time contemplating the possibility that an angel might be nearby, serving the Creator while protecting you. Or maybe you've convinced yourself that God's angels have all gone into retirement. If so, think again. God is still at work, molding His universe and guiding His believers. And He's still using angels to help accomplish His plans.

Even when we are frustrated by our inability to understand a circumstance or event, there are unseen angels bringing comfort and protection as directed by . . . God.

MARY C. NEAL

GOD'S PROMISES ABOUT ANGELS

"For the Son of man shall come
in the glory of His Father with His angels;
and then He shall reward every man according to his works."

MATTHEW 16:27 KJV

*"The harvest is the end
of the age, and the
harvesters are angels."*

MATTHEW 13:39 CSB

For He will give His angels orders concerning you,
to protect you in all your ways.

PSALM 91:11 CSB

*Praise the LORD, you angels,
you mighty ones who carry out His plans,
listening for each of His commands.*

PSALM 103:20 NLT

Are they not all ministering spirits,
sent forth to minister for them
who shall be heirs of salvation?

HEBREWS 1:14 KJV

Anger

Everyone should be quick to listen, slow to speak,
and slow to anger, for human anger
does not accomplish God's righteousness.

JAMES 1:19–20 CSB

The Bible promises that patience pays and anger costs. Anger is harmful, hurtful, and dangerous to your spiritual health. Whenever your thoughts are hijacked by angry emotions, you forfeit the peace and perspective that might otherwise be yours. And to make matters worse, angry thoughts may cause you to behave in irrational, self-destructive ways. As the old saying goes, "Anger is only one letter away from danger."

When we've been hurt badly, we don't forget easily. When we can identify the person who hurt us, we naturally focus our ire on the perpetrator. Unless we can find the inner strength to forgive that person, we're likely to internalize the anger for years, for decades, or for a lifetime. Anger turned inward is always detrimental to our spiritual health and disruptive to our lives. And that's one reason—but not the only reason—that we should learn how to forgive other people quickly and completely. To do otherwise will result in needless anger and inner turmoil.

First Peter 5:8–9 warns, "Stay alert! Watch out for your great enemy, the devil. He prowls around like a roaring lion, looking for someone to devour. Stand firm against him, and be strong in your faith" (NLT). And of this you can be sure: Your adversary will use an unforgiving heart, and the inevitable anger that dwells within it, to sabotage your life and undermine your faith. To be safe, you must cleanse your heart, and you must forgive. You must say yes to God, yes to mercy, yes to love, and no to anger.

It takes a lot of grace and maturity
to simply forgive, but a lot of healing
takes place when you do.

ELIZABETH GEORGE

GOD'S PROMISES ABOUT ANGER

"But I tell you that anyone
who is angry with a brother or sister
will be subject to judgment."

MATTHEW 5:22 NIV

He who is slow to wrath
has great understanding,
but he who is impulsive exalts folly.

PROVERBS 14:29 NKJV

A hot-tempered person stirs up conflict,
but one slow to anger calms strife.

PROVERBS 15:18 CSB

Anxiety and Worry

"Therefore do not worry about tomorrow,
for tomorrow will worry about its own things.
Sufficient for the day is its own trouble."

MATTHEW 6:34 NKJV

Because we are human beings who have the capacity to think and to anticipate future events, we worry. We worry about big things, little things, and just about everything in between. To make matters worse, we live in a world that breeds anxiety and fosters fear. So it's not surprising that when we come face to face with tough times, we may fall prey to discouragement, doubt, or depression. But our Father in heaven has other plans.

God has promised that we may lead lives of abundance, not anxiety. In fact, His Word instructs us to "be anxious for nothing." But how can we put our fears to rest? By taking those fears to Him and leaving them there.

The very same God who created the universe has promised to protect you now and forever. So what do you have to worry about? With God on your side, the answer is nothing.

Worry is like a rocking chair.
It keeps you moving
but doesn't get you anywhere.

CORRIE TEN BOOM

GOD'S PROMISES ABOUT ANXIETY AND WORRY

"Let not your heart be troubled;
you believe in God, believe also in Me."

JOHN 14:1 NKJV

***Cast all your anxiety
on Him because He cares for you.***

1 PETER 5:7 NIV

"Peace I leave with you;
My peace I give to you;
not as the world gives do I give to you.
Do not let your heart be troubled,
nor let it be fearful."

JOHN 14:27 NASB1995

***Do not be anxious about anything, but in
every situation, by prayer and petition, with
thanksgiving, present your requests to God.***

PHILIPPIANS 4:6 NIV

Cast your burden on the LORD, and He shall sustain you;
He shall never permit the righteous to be moved.

PSALM 55:22 NKJV

Asking God

"Ask, and it will be given to you;
seek, and you will find; knock, and it will be opened to you.
For every one who asks receives, and he who seeks finds,
and to him who knocks it will be opened."

MATTHEW 7:7–8 NASB1995

God invites us to ask Him for the things we need, and He promises to hear our prayers as well as our thoughts. The Lord is always available, and He's always ready to help us. And He knows precisely what we need. But He still instructs us to ask.

Do you make a habit of asking God for the things you need? Hopefully so. After all, the Father most certainly has a plan for your life. And He can do great things through you if you have the courage to ask for His guidance and His help. So be fervent in prayer and don't hesitate to ask the Creator for the tools you need to accomplish His plan for your life. Then, get busy and expect the best. When you do your part, God will most certainly do His part. And great things are bound to happen.

God will help us become the people
we are meant to be, if only we will ask Him.

HANNAH WHITALL SMITH

GOD'S PROMISES ABOUT ASKING HIM

"Until now you have asked for nothing
in My name. Ask and you will receive,
so that your joy may be complete."

JOHN 16:24 CSB

***Do not be anxious about anything,
but in every situation, by prayer and petition,
with thanksgiving, present your requests to God.***

PHILIPPIANS 4:6 NIV

The effective prayer of a righteous man
can accomplish much.

JAMES 5:16 NASB1995

***"Your Father knows the things
you have need of before you ask Him."***

MATTHEW 6:8 NKJV

"You did not choose Me, but I chose you and appointed
you so that you might go and bear fruit—
fruit that will last—and so that whatever
you ask in My name the Father will give you."

JOHN 15:16 NIV

Finally, brothers and sisters, rejoice.
Become mature, be encouraged,
be of the same mind, be at peace,
and the God of love and peace will be with you.

II CORINTHIANS 13:11 CSB

Attitudes are the mental filters through which we view and interpret the world around us. People with positive attitudes look for the best and usually find it. People burdened by chronically negative attitudes are not so fortunate.

Your attitude will inevitably determine the quality and direction of your day and your life. That's why it's so important to stay positive.

The Christian life can be, and should be, cause for celebration. After all, every new day is a gift, every new circumstance an opportunity to praise and to serve. So how will you direct your thoughts today? Will you focus on God's love? Will you hold fast to His promises and trust His plan for your life? Or will you allow your thoughts to be hijacked by negativity and doubt? If you're a thoughtful believer, you'll think optimistically about yourself and your future. And while you're at it, you'll give thanks to the Creator for more blessings than you can count.

Attitude is

the mind's paintbrush;

it can color

any situation.

BARBARA JOHNSON

GOD'S PROMISES ABOUT ATTITUDE

A merry heart makes
a cheerful countenance.
PROVERBS 15:13 NKJV

You must have the same attitude
that Christ Jesus had.
PHILIPPIANS 2:5 NLT

"Be glad and rejoice,
because your reward
is great in heaven."
MATTHEW 5:12 CSB

Rejoice always; pray without ceasing.
I THESSALONIANS 5:16–17 NASB

This is the day the LORD has made;
let's rejoice and be glad in it.
PSALM 118:24 CSB

Beliefs

"I have come as a light into the world, that whoever believes in Me should not abide in darkness."

JOHN 12:46 NKJV

Talking about our beliefs is easy; living by them is considerably harder. Yet God warns us that speaking about faith is not enough; we must also live by faith. Simply put, our theology must be demonstrated, not only with words but, more importantly, with actions.

As Christians, our instructions are clear: we should trust God's plan, obey God's Word, and follow God's Son. When we do these things, we inevitably partake in the spiritual abundance that the Creator has promised to those who walk in the light. But if we listen to God's instructions on Sunday morning and ignore them the rest of the week, we'll pay a heavy price for our misplaced priorities.

Every new day presents fresh opportunities to ensure that your actions are consistent with your beliefs. Seize those opportunities. Now.

Only believe, don't fear. Our Master, Jesus, always watches over us, and no matter what the persecution, Jesus will surely overcome it.

LOTTIE MOON

GOD'S PROMISES ABOUT BELIEFS

Jesus said, "Because you have seen Me,
you have believed. Blessed are those
who have not seen and yet believe."

JOHN 20:29 CSB

*"I tell you the truth, whoever believes in Me
will do the same things that I do.
Those who believe will do even greater things
than these, because I am going to the Father."*

JOHN 14:12 NCV

"Most assuredly, I say to you, he who
believes in Me, the works that I do he will do also."

JOHN 14:12 NKJV

*"All things are possible
for the one who believes."*

MARK 9:23 NCV

I know Whom I have believed
and am persuaded that He is able
to guard what has been
entrusted to me until that day.

II TIMOTHY 1:12 CSB

The Bible

For the word of God is living and effective and sharper than any double-edged sword, penetrating as far as the separation of soul and spirit, joints and marrow. It is able to judge the thoughts and intentions of the heart.

HEBREWS 4:12 CSB

The promises found in God's Word are the cornerstone of the Christian faith. We must trust those promises and build our lives upon them.

The Bible is a priceless gift—a tool for Christians to use every day, in every situation. Yet too many Christians put away their spiritual tool kits and rely instead on the world's promises. Unfortunately, the world makes promises it doesn't keep. God has no such record of failure. He keeps every single one of His promises. On Him you can depend.

So how will you respond to God's promises? Will you treat your Bible as a one-of-a-kind guidebook for life here on earth and life eternal in heaven? Hopefully so because the Lord has given you all the tools you need to accomplish His plan for your life. He placed every instruction you'll need in the book He wrote. The rest is up to you.

God's Word is a map you can safely follow as you travel through life.

ELIZABETH GEORGE

GOD'S PROMISES ABOUT THE BIBLE

All Scripture is given by
inspiration of God,
and is profitable for doctrine,
for reproof, for correction,
for instruction in righteousness.

II TIMOTHY 3:16 KJV

"Therefore everyone who hears these words of Mine and puts them into practice is like a wise man who built his house on the rock."

MATTHEW 7:24 NIV

Jesus answered, "It is written:
'Man shall not live on bread alone,
but on every word that comes
from the mouth of God.'"

MATTHEW 4:4 NIV

Your word is a lamp for my feet and a light on my path.

PSALM 119:105 CSB

Blessings

May the LORD bless you and protect you;
may the LORD make His face shine on you,
and be gracious to you.

NUMBERS 6:24–25 CSB

If you tried to count all your blessings, how long would it take? A very, very long time. After all, you've been given the priceless gift of life here on earth and the promise of life eternal in heaven. And you've been given so much more.

Life itself, every bit of health that we enjoy, every hour of liberty and free enjoyment, the ability to see, to hear, to speak, to think, and to imagine- all this comes from the hand of God. We show our gratitude by giving back to Him a part of that which He has given to us. That's sound advice for believers—followers of the One from Galilee—who have so much to be thankful for.

Your blessings, all of which are gifts from above, are indeed too numerous to count, but it never hurts to begin counting them anyway. It never hurts to say thanks to the Giver for the gifts you can count, and all the other ones too.

God is the giver,

and we are the receivers.

And His riches are gifted

not upon those

who do the greatest things,

but upon those who accept

His abundance and His grace.

HANNAH WHITALL SMITH

GOD'S PROMISES ABOUT BLESSINGS

You will show me the
path of life; in Your presence
is fullness of joy;
at Your right hand are
pleasures forevermore.

PSALM 16:11 NKJV

The Lord is good to all:
and His tender mercies are over all His works.

PSALM 145:9 KJV

The Lord is my rock, my fortress,
and my deliverer, my God, my rock where I seek refuge.
My shield, the horn of my salvation,
my stronghold, my refuge, and my Savior.

II SAMUEL 22:2–3 CSB

The Lord is my shepherd; I shall not want.

PSALM 23:1 KJV

Blessings crown the
head of the righteous.

PROVERBS 10:6 NIV

Busyness

Return unto thy rest, O my soul;
for the LORD hath dealt bountifully with thee.

PSALM 116:7 KJV

For most of us, life is busy, perhaps too busy for our own good. We rush from place to place, with scarcely a moment to spare, checking smart phones along the way. Meanwhile, we're constantly bombarded by a steady stream of media, much of it disturbing. No wonder we're stressed!

Has the busy pace of twenty-first-century life robbed you of the peace and serenity that could otherwise be yours through Jesus Christ? If so, it's time to slow down, do less, and appreciate life a little more.

As you consider your priorities, remember that time with God is paramount. You owe it to yourself to spend time each day with your Creator, seeking His guidance and studying His Word. Those quiet moments of prayer and meditation are invaluable. When you let God help you organize your day, you'll find that He'll give you the time and the tools to do the most important tasks on your to-do list. And what about all those less important things on your list? Perhaps they're best left undone.

Strength is found not in busyness
and noise but in quietness.

LETTIE COWMAN

GOD'S PROMISES ABOUT BUSYNESS

"Come unto Me, all ye that labour
and are heavy laden,
and I will give you rest."
MATTHEW 11:28 KJV

*In quietness and in confidence
shall be your strength.*
ISAIAH 30:15 KJV

Be still before the LORD
and wait patiently for Him.
PSALM 37:7 NIV

*Rest in God alone, my soul,
for my hope comes from Him.*
PSALM 62:5 CSB

And the peace of God,
which surpasses
all comprehension,
will guard your hearts
and your minds in Christ Jesus.
PHILIPPIANS 4:7 NASB1995

Celebration

Rejoice in the Lord always.
Again I will say, rejoice!
PHILIPPIANS 4:4 NKJV

Each day contains cause for celebration. And each day has its own share of blessings. Our assignment, as grateful believers, is to look for the blessings and celebrate them.

Today, like every other day, is a priceless gift from God. He has offered us yet another opportunity to serve Him with smiling faces and willing hands. When we do our part, He inevitably does His part, and miracles happen.

The Lord has promised to bless you and keep you, now and forever. So, don't wait for birthdays or holidays. Make this day an exciting adventure. And while you're at it, take time to thank God for His blessings. He deserves your thanks, and you deserve the joy of expressing it.

Joy is the settled assurance that God
is in control of all the details of my life,
the quiet confidence that ultimately
everything is going to be all right, and the
determined choice to praise God in all things.

KAY WARREN

GOD'S PROMISES ABOUT CELEBRATION

A happy heart is
like a continual feast.

PROVERBS 15:15 NCV

*This is the day which
the LORD has made;
let us rejoice and be glad in it.*

PSALM 118:24 NASB1995

Rejoice always, pray without ceasing,
in everything give thanks; for this is the will
of God in Christ Jesus for you.

1 THESSALONIANS 5:16–18 NKJV

*I delight greatly in the LORD;
my soul rejoices in my God.*

ISAIAH 61:10 NIV

"I came that they may have life,
and have it abundantly."

JOHN 10:10 NASB1995

Charity and Generosity

"Freely you have received; freely give."

MATTHEW 10:8 NIV

The theme of generosity is woven into the fabric of God's Word. Our Creator instructs us to give generously—and cheerfully—to those in need. And He promises that when we do give of our time, our talents, and our resources, we will be blessed.

Jesus was the perfect example of generosity. He gave us everything, even His earthly life, so that we, His followers, might receive abundance, peace, and eternal life. He was always generous, always kind, always willing to help "the least of these." And, if we are to follow in His footsteps, we too must be generous.

Sometime today you'll encounter someone who needs a helping hand or a word of encouragement. When you encounter a person in need, think of yourself as Christ's ambassador. And remember that whatever you do for the least of these, you also do for Him.

No matter how little you have,
you can always give some of it away.

CATHERINE MARSHALL

GOD'S PROMISES ABOUT CHARITY AND GENEROSITY

So let each one give as he purposes in his heart,
not grudgingly or of necessity;
for God loves a cheerful giver.

II CORINTHIANS 9:7 NKJV

***You should remember
the words of the Lord Jesus:
"It is more blessed to give than to receive."***

ACTS 20:35 NLT

If you have two shirts, give one to the poor.
If you have food, share it with those
who are hungry.

LUKE 3:11 NLT

***Whenever we have the opportunity,
we should do good to everyone—
especially to those in the family of faith.***

GALATIANS 6:10 NLT

The King will reply, 'Truly I tell you,
whatever you did for one of the least of these
brothers and sisters of Mine, you did for Me.'

MATTHEW 25:40 NIV

Cheerfulness

A cheerful heart has a continual feast.

PROVERBS 15:15 CSB

As Christians, we have so many reasons to be cheerful: God is in His heaven; He remains firmly in control; He loves us; and through His Son He has offered us a path to eternal life. Despite these blessings, all of us will occasionally fall victim to the inevitable frustrations of everyday life. When we do, we should pause, take a deep breath, and remember how richly we've been blessed.

Cheerfulness is a gift that we give to others and to ourselves. The joy we give to others is reciprocal: whatever we give away is returned to us, oftentimes in greater measure. So make this promise to yourself and keep it: be a cheerful ambassador for Christ. He deserves no less, and neither, for that matter, do you.

The happiness which God designs for his higher creatures is the happiness of being freely, voluntarily united to Him.

C.S. LEWIS

GOD'S PROMISES ABOUT CHEERFULNESS

Rejoice always, pray without ceasing,
in everything give thanks; for this
is the will of God in Christ Jesus for you.

I THESSALONIANS 5:16–18 NKJV

This is the day that
the Lord has made.
Let us rejoice and
be glad today!

PSALM 118:24 NCV

Shout for joy to the Lord, all the earth.
Worship the Lord with gladness;
come before Him with joyful songs.

PSALM 100:1–2 NIV

Do everything without grumbling and arguing,
so that you may be blameless and pure.

PHILIPPIANS 2:14–15 CSB

A cheerful heart is good medicine,
but a crushed spirit dries up the bones.

PROVERBS 17:22 NIV

Christ's Love

"As the Father loved Me,
I also have loved you;
abide in My love."
JOHN 15:9 NKJV

Jesus loves us so much that He willingly sacrificed Himself on the cross so that we might live with Him throughout eternity. His love endures. Even when we falter, He loves us. When we fall prey to the world's temptations, He remains steadfast. In fact, no power on earth can separate us from His love.

Christ can transform us. When we open our hearts to Him and walk in His footsteps, our lives bear testimony to His mercy and to His grace. Yes, Christ's love changes everything. May we welcome Him into our hearts so that He can then change everything in us.

Jesus is all compassion.
He never betrays us.
CATHERINE MARSHALL

GOD'S PROMISES ABOUT CHRIST'S LOVE

"I am the good shepherd.
The good shepherd
lays down His life for the sheep."
JOHN 10:11 CSB

*"No one has greater love than this:
to lay down his life for his friends."*
JOHN 15:13 CSB

For Christ also suffered once for sins,
the just for the unjust, that He might
bring us to God, being put to death
in the flesh but made alive by the Spirit.
I PETER 3:18 NKJV

We love Him, because He first loved us.
I JOHN 4:19 KJV

"For God so loved the world,
that He gave His only begotten Son,
that whosoever believeth in Him should not perish,
but have everlasting life."
JOHN 3:16 KJV

Circumstances

Trust in Him at all times, O people;
pour out your hearts to Him,
for God is our refuge.

PSALM 62:8 NIV

From time to time, all of us must endure unpleasant circumstances. We find ourselves in situations that we didn't ask for and probably don't deserve. During these times, we try our best to "hold up under the circumstances." But God has a better plan: He intends for us to rise *above* our circumstances, and He's promised to help us do it.

Are you dealing with a difficult situation or a tough problem? Do you struggle with occasional periods of discouragement and doubt? Are you worried, weary, or downcast? If so, don't face tough times alone. Face them with God as your partner, your protector, and your guide. When you do, He will give you the strength to meet any challenge, the courage to face any problem, and the patience to endure any circumstance.

Today I know that such memories are the key not to the past, but to the future. I know that the experiences of our lives, when we let God use them, become the mysterious and perfect preparation for the work he will give us to do.

CORRIE TEN BOOM

GOD'S PROMISES ABOUT CIRCUMSTANCES

The LORD is a refuge for His people
and a stronghold.

JOEL 3:16 NASB

The LORD is a refuge for
the persecuted,
a refuge in times of trouble.

PSALM 9:9 CSB

Cast your burden on the LORD,
and He shall sustain you; He shall never
permit the righteous to be moved.

PSALM 55:22 NKJV

God is our protection
and our strength.
He always helps in
times of trouble.

PSALM 46:1 NCV

I have learned in whatever state I am,
to be content.

PHILIPPIANS 4:11 NKJV

Comforting Others

Therefore, as God's chosen ones,
holy and dearly loved put on heartfelt compassion,
kindness, humility, gentleness, and patience.

COLOSSIANS 3:12 CSB

The world can be a dangerous and discouraging place, a place where real people experience real problems and real pain. When they do, we are presented with real opportunities to offer comfort. God wants us to seize those opportunities early and often.

Wherever you go, you'll encounter people who need your encouragement. Today, when you encounter someone who needs a comforting word, a pat on the back, a hug, or a helping hand, be quick to respond. You possess the power to make the world a better place one person at a time. When you use that power wisely, you make your own corner of the world a kinder, gentler, happier place.

God's Word instructs us to be kind and helpful, especially to those in need. So as you make your plans for the day ahead, look for people to comfort and people to help. When you do, you'll be a powerful example to others *and* a worthy servant to your Creator.

The measure of a life,

after all,

is not its duration

but its donation.

CORRIE TEN BOOM

GOD'S PROMISES ABOUT COMFORTING OTHERS

Let us think about each other and help
each other to show love and do good deeds.

HEBREWS 10:24 NCV

Do not withhold good from those to whom it is due, when it is within your power to act.

PROVERBS 3:27 NIV

"Do to others as you
would have them do to you."

LUKE 6:31 NIV

So let's not get tired of
doing what is good.
At just the right time
we will reap
a harvest of blessing
if we don't give up.

GALATIANS 6:9 NLT

Carry one another's burdens;
in this way you will fulfill the law of Christ.

GALATIANS 6:2 CSB

Confidence

So we may boldly say:
"The LORD is my helper; I will not fear.
What can man do to me?"

HEBREWS 13:6 NKJV

As Christians, we have every reason to live confidently. After all, we've read God's promises and we know that He's prepared a place for us in heaven. And with God on our side, what should we fear? The answer, of course, is nothing. But sometimes, despite our faith and despite God's promises, we find ourselves gripped by earthly apprehensions.

When we focus on our doubts and fears, we can concoct a lengthy list of reasons to lie awake at night and fret about the uncertainties of the coming day. A better strategy, of course, is to focus, not upon our fears, but upon our God.

Are you a confident Christian? You should be. God's promises never fail, and His love is everlasting. So the next time you need a boost of confidence, slow down and have a little chat with your Creator. Count your blessings, not your troubles. Focus on possibilities, not problems. And remember that with God on your side, you have absolutely nothing to fear.

Faith in God is the

greatest power,

but great, too,

is faith in oneself.

MARY MCLEOD BETHUNE

GOD'S PROMISES ABOUT CONFIDENCE

You are my hope; O Lord GOD,
You are my confidence.
PSALM 71:5 NASB1995

I lift up my eyes to the mountains—
where does my help come from? My help comes
from the LORD, the Maker of heaven and earth.
PSALM 121:1–2 NIV

God is our refuge and strength,
a very present help in trouble.
PSALM 46:1 NKJV

Be strong and courageous,
and do the work.
Don't be afraid or discouraged,
for the LORD God, my God, is with you.
He won't leave you or abandon you.
1 CHRONICLES 28:20 CSB

"In this world you will have trouble.
But take heart! I have overcome the world."
JOHN 16:33 NIV

Contentment

I have learned in whatever state I am, to be content.

PHILIPPIANS 4:11 NKJV

The Bible promises that contentment can be ours if we honor God's commandments and follow, as closely as we can, in the footsteps of His Son. But the world seeks to sell you a different brand of contentment. The world promises that "happiness and serenity" can be purchased...at the right price. The world's marketers perpetuate the misconception that lasting satisfaction is for sale at the local mall, but nothing could be further from the truth. Genuine peace is not for sale at any price.

So where will you find contentment today? Will you trust God to provide it, or will you expect the world to do the job? If you expect the world to provide a sense of serenity and peace, you'll be disappointed sooner or later (probably sooner). But if you turn your heart and your life over to the One from Galilee, you'll be blessed now (and forever)...and you'll be content.

No matter what you're facing,
embrace life in trust and contentment
based on your faith in Jesus.

ELIZABETH GEORGE

GOD'S PROMISES ABOUT CONTENTMENT

But godliness with
contentment is a great gain.

I TIMOTHY 6:6 CSB

Make sure that your character is free from the love of money, being content with what you have; for He Himself has said, "I will never desert you, nor will I ever abandon you."

HEBREWS 13:5 NASB

A tranquil heart is life to the body,
but jealousy is rottenness to the bones.

PROVERBS 14:30 CSB

***"Come unto Me,
all ye that labour
and are heavy laden,
and I will give you rest."***

MATTHEW 11:28 KJV

The peace of God, which passeth all understanding, shall keep your hearts and minds through Christ Jesus.

PHILIPPIANS 4:7 KJV

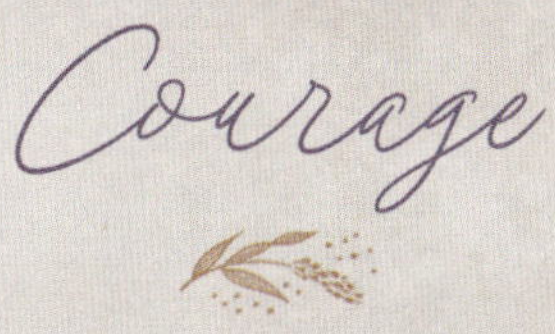

Courage

Be strong and courageous, and do the work.
Do not be afraid or discouraged,
for the LORD God, my God, is with you.

I CHRONICLES 28:20 NIV

As believers in a risen Christ, we can, and should, live courageously. After all, Jesus promises us that He has overcome the world and that He has made a place for us in heaven. So we have nothing to fear in the long term because our Lord will care for us throughout eternity. But what about those short-term, everyday worries that keep us up at night? And what about the life-altering hardships that leave us wondering if we can ever recover? The answer, of course, is that because God cares for us in good times and hard times, we can turn our concerns over to Him in prayer, knowing that all things ultimately work for the good of those who love Him.

When you form a one-on-one relationship with your Creator, you can be comforted by the fact that wherever you find yourself, whether at the top of the mountain or the depths of the valley, God is there with you. And because your Creator cares for you and protects you, you can rise above your fears.

At this very moment the Lord is seeking to work in you and through you. He's asking you to live abundantly and courageously, and He's ready to help. So why not let Him do it... starting now?

Just as courage

is faith in good,

so discouragement is faith in evil;

and, while courage

opens the door to good,

discouragement opens it to evil.

HANNAH WHITALL SMITH

GOD'S PROMISES ABOUT COURAGE

Be on guard. Stand firm in the faith.
Be courageous. Be strong.

I CORINTHIANS 16:13 NLT

For God has not given us a spirit of fear, but one of power, love, and sound judgment.

II TIMOTHY 1:7 CSB

I can do all things through
Him who strengthens me.

PHILIPPIANS 4:13 NASB

But He said to them, "It is I; do not be afraid."

JOHN 6:20 NKJV

Behold, God is my salvation;
I will trust, and not be afraid.

ISAIAH 12:2 KJV

Decisions

But if any of you needs wisdom,
you should ask God for it.
He is generous to everyone
and will give you wisdom
without criticizing you.
JAMES 1:5 NCV

Each day you must make countless decisions. Many of those decisions are so tightly woven into the fabric of your life that you scarcely realize that they are decisions at all. Other decisions are made purely out of habit. But occasionally you'll find yourself at one of life's inevitable crossroads, and when you do, it's time to slow down and have a heart-to-heart talk with the ultimate Counselor: your Father in heaven.

The Bible offers clear guidance about decision-making. So, if you're about to make an important decision, here are some things you can do:

1. Gather information. Don't expect to get all the facts—that's impossible—but try to gather as much information as you can in a reasonable amount of time (Proverbs 24:3–4).

2. Be patient. If you have time to make a decision, use that time to make a good decision (Proverbs 19:2).
3. Rely on the counsel of a few friends and mentors. Proverbs 1:5 makes it clear: "A wise man will hear and increase learning, and a man of understanding will attain wise counsel" (NKJV).
4. Pray for guidance and listen carefully to your conscience.
5. When the time for action arrives, act. Procrastination is the enemy of progress; don't let it defeat you (James 1:22).

There may be no trumpet sound
or loud applause when we make a right decision,
just a calm sense of resolution and peace.

GLORIA GAITHER

GOD'S PROMISES ABOUT DECISIONS

In every way be an example
of doing good deeds.
When you teach,
do it with honesty and seriousness.

TITUS 2:7 NCV

We can make our own plans,
but the LORD gives the right answer.
People may be pure in their own eyes,
but the LORD examines their motives.

PROVERBS 16:1–2 NLT

Blessed is the man who walks
not in the counsel of the ungodly,
nor stands in the path of sinners,
nor sits in the seat of the scornful.

PSALM 1:1 NKJV

Whether you turn to the right or to the left,
your ears will hear a voice behind you, saying,
"This is the way; walk in it."

ISAIAH 30:21 NIV

Devotions

Morning by morning He wakens me
and opens my understanding to His will.
The Sovereign LORD has spoken to me,
and I have listened.

ISAIAH 50:4-5 NLT

Every new day is a gift from the Creator, a gift that allows each of us to say "thank You" by spending time with the Giver. When we begin the day with our Bibles open and our hearts attuned to God, we are inevitably blessed by the promises we find in His Word.

Each day has 1,440 minutes. God deserves a few of those minutes. And you deserve the experience of spending a few quiet minutes with your Creator. So, if you haven't already done so, establish the habit of spending time with your Creator every day of the week. It's a habit that will change your day and revolutionize your life.

Begin each day with God.
It will change your priorities.

ELIZABETH GEORGE

GOD'S PROMISES ABOUT DEVOTIONS

It is good to give thanks to the LORD,
And to sing praises to Your name, O Most High.

PSALM 92:1 NKJV

"Heaven and earth will pass away,
but My words will never pass away."

MATTHEW 24:35 CSB

Thy word is a lamp unto my feet,
and a light unto my path.

PSALM 119:105 KJV

Early the next morning, while it was still dark,
Jesus woke and left the house.
He went to a lonely place, where He prayed.

MARK 1:35 NCV

But grow in the grace and
knowledge of our Lord
and Savior Jesus Christ.
To Him be the glory both
now and to the day of eternity.

II PETER 3:18 CSB

Disappointments

Then they cried out to the LORD in their trouble,
and He saved them out of their distresses.

PSALM 107:13 NKJV

As we make the journey from the cradle to the grave, disappointments are inevitable. No matter how competent we are, no matter how fortunate, we still encounter circumstances that fall far short of our expectations. When tough times arrive, we have choices to make: we can feel sorry for ourselves, or we can get angry, or we can become depressed. Or, we can get busy praying about our problems and solving them.

When we are disheartened—on those cloudy days when our strength is sapped and our hope is shaken—there exists a source from which we can draw perspective and courage. That source is God. When we turn everything over to Him, we find that He is sufficient to meet our needs. No problem is too big for Him.

So, the next time you feel discouraged, slow down long enough to have a serious talk with your Creator. Pray for guidance, pray for strength, and pray for the wisdom to trust your heavenly Father. Your troubles are temporary; His love is not.

Allow God to use
the difficulties and
disappointments
in life as polish to transform
your faith into a glistening
diamond that takes
in and reflects His love.

ELIZABETH GEORGE

GOD'S PROMISES ABOUT DISAPPOINTMENTS

He heals the brokenhearted
and bandages their wounds.

PSALM 147:3 CSB

*He shall not be afraid of evil tidings:
his heart is fixed, trusting in the LORD.*

PSALM 112:7 KJV

One who is righteous has many adversities,
but the LORD rescues him from them all.

PSALM 34:19 CSB

*My son, do not despise the
chastening of the LORD, nor be discouraged
when you are rebuked by Him.*

HEBREWS 12:5 NKJV

They that sow in tears shall reap in joy.

PSALM 126:5 KJV

Dreams

When dreams come true . . . there is life and joy.

PROVERBS 13:12 TLB

Do you consider the future to be friend or foe? Do you expect the best, and are you willing to work for it? If so, please consider the fact that the Lord does, indeed, help those who help themselves. And He's especially helpful to those who consult Him before they finalize their plans.

God's help is always available to those who ask. Our job, of course, is to seek His guidance and His strength as we seek to accomplish His plans for our lives.

Nothing is too difficult for God, and no dreams are too big for Him—not even yours. When you do your part, He'll do His part, and great things are bound to happen. So live confidently, plan carefully, do your best, and leave the rest up to the Creator. You and He, working together, can move mountains. Lots of them.

When the dream of our heart is one that God has planted there, a strange happiness flows into us. At that moment, the spiritual resources of the universe are released to help us.

CATHERINE MARSHALL

GOD'S PROMISES ABOUT DREAMS

Hope deferred makes the heart sick,
But when the desire comes,
it is a tree of life.
PROVERBS 13:12 NKJV

Where there is no vision, the people perish.
PROVERBS 29:18 KJV

But we are hoping for
something we do not have yet,
and we are waiting for it patiently.
ROMANS 8:25 NCV

Now may the God of hope
fill you with all joy and peace
as you believe so that you may overflow
with hope by the power of the Holy Spirit.
ROMANS 15:13 CSB

Humble yourselves therefore
under the mighty hand
of God, that He may exalt you in due time.
I PETER 5:6 KJV

Encouragement

But encourage each other daily,
while it is still called today, so that none of you
is hardened by sin's deception.

HEBREWS 3:13 CSB

Whether we realize it or not, all of us need encouragement. The world can be a difficult place, a place where we encounter the inevitable disappointments that are woven into the fabric of everyday life. So we all need boosters who are ready, willing, and able to cheer us on when times get tough.

God's Word teaches that we must treat others as we ourselves wish to be treated. Since we desire encouragement for ourselves, we should be quick to share it with others.

Whom will you encourage today? How many times will you share a smile, or a kind word, or a pat on the back? You'll probably have many opportunities to share the gift of encouragement. When you seize those opportunities, others will be blessed, and you'll be blessed too. But not necessarily in that order.

Developing a positive attitude
means working continually
to find what is uplifting and encouraging.

BARBARA JOHNSON

GOD'S PROMISES ABOUT ENCOURAGEMENT

Let us think about each other
and help each other to show
love and do good deeds.

HEBREWS 10:24 ICB

*Bear one another's burdens,
and so fulfill the law of Christ.*

GALATIANS 6:2 NKJV

So encourage each other
and give each other strength,
just as you are doing now.

I THESSALONIANS 5:11 NCV

*When you talk, do not say harmful things,
but say what people need—words that will
help others become stronger. Then what you
say will do good to those who listen to you.*

EPHESIANS 4:29 NCV

Now we exhort you, brethren, warn those
who are unruly, comfort the fainthearted,
uphold the weak, be patient with all.

I THESSALONIANS 5:14 NKJV

Enthusiasm

Whatever you do, do it from the heart
as something done for the Lord and not for people.

COLOSSIANS 3:23 CSB

As a woman who's striving to follow in the footsteps of God's Son, you have many reasons to be enthusiastic about your life, your opportunities, and your future. After all, your eternal destiny is secure. Christ died for your sins, and He wants you to experience life abundant and life eternal. So what's not to get excited about?

Are you a passionate person and an enthusiastic Christian? Are you genuinely excited about your faith, your family, and your future? Hopefully you can answer these questions with a resounding yes. But if your passion for life has waned, it's time to slow down long enough to recharge your spiritual batteries and reorder your priorities.

Each new day is an opportunity to put God first and celebrate His creation. Today, take time to count your blessings and take stock of your opportunities. And while you're at it, ask God for strength. When you sincerely petition Him, He will give you everything you need to live enthusiastically and abundantly.

If you can forgive
the person you were,
accept the person you are,
and believe in the person
you will become,
you are headed for joy.
So celebrate your life.

BARBARA JOHNSON

GOD'S PROMISES ABOUT ENTHUSIASM

Do your work with enthusiasm.
Work as if you were serving
the Lord, not as if you were
serving only men and women.

EPHESIANS 6:7 NCV

*A happy heart makes the face cheerful,
but heartache crushes the spirit.*

PROVERBS 15:13 NIV

But as for me, I will hope continually,
and will praise You yet more and more.

PSALM 71:14 NASB1995

*Rejoice always, pray constantly,
give thanks in everything;
for this is God's will for you in Christ Jesus.*

I THESSALONIANS 5:16–18 CSB

Let the hearts of those
who seek the LORD rejoice.
Look to the Lord and His strength;
seek His face always.

I CHRONICLES 16:10–11 NIV

Envy

Let us not be desirous of vainglory,
provoking one another, envying one another.

GALATIANS 5:26 KJV

God's Word warns us about a dangerous, destructive state of mind: envy. Envy is emotional poison. It poisons the mind and hardens the heart.

If we are to experience the abundant lives that Christ has promised, we must be on guard against envious thoughts. Jealousy breeds discontent, discontent breeds unhappiness, and unhappiness robs us of the peace that might otherwise be ours.

So if the sin of envy has invaded your heart, ask God to help you heal. When you ask sincerely and often, He will respond. And when He does, you'll regain the peace that can only be found through Him.

The things we think are the things that feed our souls.
If we think on pure and lovely things,
we shall grow pure and lovely like them;
and the converse is equally true.

HANNAH WHITALL SMITH

GOD'S PROMISES ABOUT ENVY

Therefore, rid yourselves of all malice,
all deceit, hypocrisy,
envy, and all slander.

I PETER 2:1 CSB

You must not covet your neighbor's house.
You must not covet your neighbor's wife,
male or female servant, ox or donkey,
or anything else that belongs to your neighbor.

EXODUS 20:17 NLT

Let us not become boastful,
challenging one another,
envying one another.

GALATIANS 5:26 NASB1995

Where jealousy and selfishness are,
there will be confusion and every kind of evil.

JAMES 3:16 NCV

Don't envy the evil or
desire to be with them.

PROVERBS 24:1 CSB

Eternal Life

"For God so loved the world,
that He gave His only begotten Son,
that whosoever believeth in Him should
not perish, but have everlasting life."

JOHN 3:16 KJV

Jesus is not only the light of the world; He is also its salvation. He came to this earth so that we might not perish but instead spend eternity with Him. What a glorious gift; what a priceless opportunity.

As mere mortals, we cannot fully understand the scope, and thus the value, of eternal life. Our vision is limited but God's is not. He sees all things; He knows all things; and His plans for you extend throughout eternity.

If you haven't already done so, this moment is the perfect moment to turn your life over to God's only begotten Son. When you give your heart to the Son, you belong to the Father—today, tomorrow, and for all eternity.

Eternal life does not start when we go to heaven. It starts the moment you reach out to Jesus. He never turns His back on anyone. And He is waiting for you.

CORRIE TEN BOOM

GOD'S PROMISES ABOUT ETERNAL LIFE

"Truly I tell you, anyone who hears
My word and believes Him who sent
Me has eternal life and will not come
under judgment but has passed from death to life."

JOHN 5:24 CSB

*For the wages of sin is death, but the gift of God
is eternal life in Christ Jesus our Lord.*

ROMANS 6:23 NIV

I have written these things to you who believe
in the name of the Son of God
so that you may know that
you have eternal life.

I JOHN 5:13 CSB

*The world and its desires pass away,
but whoever does the will of God lives forever.*

I JOHN 2:17 NIV

The last enemy that
will be destroyed is death.

I CORINTHIANS 15:26 NKJV

Faith

"For truly I say to you, if you have faith the size of a mustard seed, you will say to this mountain, 'Move from here to there,' and it will move; and nothing will be impossible to you."

MATTHEW 17:20 NASB1995

The Bible makes it clear: faith is powerful. With it, we can move mountains. With it, we can endure any hardship. With it, we can rise above the challenges of everyday life and live victoriously, whatever our circumstances.

Is your faith strong enough to move the mountains in your own life? If so, you're already tapped in to a source of strength that never fails: God's strength. But if your spiritual batteries are in need of recharging, don't be discouraged. God's strength is always available to those who seek.

The first element of a successful life is faith: faith in God, faith in His promises, and faith in His Son. When our faith in the Creator is strong, we can then have faith in ourselves, knowing that we are tools in the hands of a loving God who made mountains—and moves them—according to a perfect plan that only He can see.

I beg you to recognize
the extreme simplicity of faith.
I beg you to recognize that
it is nothing more nor less than
just believing God when
He says He either has done
something for us, or will do it.
Then trust Him to keep His word.
It is so simple that
it is hard to explain.

HANNAH WHITALL SMITH

GOD'S PROMISES ABOUT FAITH

Don't be afraid,
because I am your God.
I will make you strong and will help you;
I will support you with My
right hand that saves you.

ISAIAH 41:10 NCV

"Don't be afraid. Only believe."

MARK 5:36 CSB

"Blessed are they that have not seen,
and yet have believed."

JOHN 20:29 KJV

*"All things are possible
for the one who believes."*

MARK 9:23 NCV

And He said unto her,
"Daughter, thy faith
hath made thee whole;
go in peace, and be whole."

MARK 5:34 KJV

Choose for yourselves this day whom you will serve....
But as for me and my house, we will serve the LORD.

JOSHUA 24:15 NKJV

Our families are a gift from the Creator. God, in His infinite wisdom, has placed us precisely where we need to be to fulfill a plan that only He can see. Our families are a part of that plan, so we should be grateful, and we must never take our loved ones for granted.

When someone asked Mother Teresa how best to promote world peace, she said, "Go home and love your family."

Someone in your family probably needs help today. And everybody in your family needs love today. Or they need a word of encouragement. Or a pat on the back. Or a hug. Whether you realize it or not, the needs are great. And the next move is yours.

Line by line, moment by moment, special times are etched into our memories in the permanent ink of everlasting love in our relationships.

GLORIA GAITHER

GOD'S PROMISES ABOUT FAMILY

"Every kingdom divided against itself
is headed for destruction,
and a house divided against itself falls."

LUKE 11:17 CSB

*But if anyone does not provide
for his own, and especially
for those of his household, he has denied the
faith and is worse than an unbeliever.*

I TIMOTHY 5:8 NASB

Better a dry crust with peace
than a house full of feasting with strife.

PROVERBS 17:1 CSB

*Their first responsibility is to show godliness
at home and repay their parents by taking care
of them. This is something that pleases God.*

I TIMOTHY 5:4 NLT

But now faith, hope, love,
abide these three;
but the greatest of these is love.

I CORINTHIANS 13:13 NASB1995

Fear

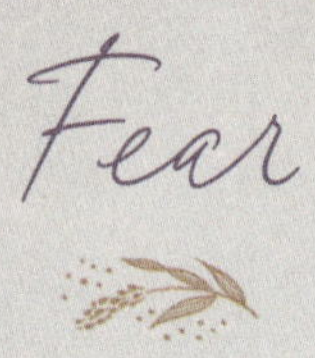

"Peace I leave with you; My peace I give to you;
not as the world gives do I give to you.
Do not let your heart be troubled, nor let it be fearful."

JOHN 14:27 NASB1995

From time to time, all of us experience difficult days when unexpected circumstances test our mettle. When these situations occur, fear creeps in and threatens to overtake our minds and our hearts.

Difficult times call for courageous measures. Running away from problems only perpetuates them; fear begets more fear; and anxiety is a poor counselor. As Maya Angelou observed, "Fear brings out the worst in everybody."

Adversity visits everyone—no human being is beyond Old Man Trouble's reach. But Old Man Trouble is not just an unwelcome guest; he is also an invaluable teacher. If we are to become mature human beings, it is our duty to learn from the inevitable hardships and heartbreaks of life.

Today, ask God to help you step beyond the boundaries of your fear. Ask Him to guide you to a place where you can realize your potential—a place where you are freed from the paralysis of anxiety. Ask Him to do His part, and then promise Him that you'll do your part. Don't ask God to lead you to a safe place; ask Him to lead you to the right place. And remember that those two places are seldom the same.

When fears regarding the cares of this world set in, we need to confidently lean on God's promise to care for us.

ELIZABETH GEORGE

GOD'S PROMISES ABOUT FEAR

But He said to them,
"It is I; do not be afraid."
JOHN 6:20 NKJV

"Fear not, for I am with you;
be not dismayed, for I am your God.
I will strengthen you, yes,
I will help you, I will uphold you
with My righteous right hand."
ISAIAH 41:10 NKJV

The LORD is my light and my salvation—
whom should I fear?
The LORD is the stronghold of my life—
of whom should I dread?
PSALM 27:1 CSB

Even though I walk through the darkest valley,
I will fear no evil, for You are with me;
Your rod and Your staff, they comfort me.
PSALM 23:4 NIV

"Be not afraid, only believe."
MARK 5:36 KJV

Following Christ

Then He said to them all, "If anyone wants
to follow after Me, let him deny himself,
take up his cross daily, and follow Me."

LUKE 9:23 CSB

Every day, we're presented with countless opportunities to honor God by following in the footsteps of His Son. But we're sorely tempted to do otherwise. The world is filled to the brim with temptations and distractions that beckon us down a different path.

Elisabeth Elliot had this advice for believers everywhere: "Choose Jesus Christ! Deny yourself, take up the cross, and follow Him—for the world must be shown. The world must see, in us, a discernible, visible, startling difference."

Today, do your part to take up your cross and follow Him, even if the world encourages you to do otherwise. When you're traveling step-by-step with the Son of God, you're always on the right path.

This my song through endless ages,
Jesus led me all the way.

FANNY CROSBY

GOD'S PROMISES ABOUT FOLLOWING CHRIST

But whoever keeps His word, truly in him the love of God is made complete. This is how we know we are in Him: the one who says he remains in Him should walk just as He walked.

I JOHN 2:5–6 CSB

Walk in a manner worthy of the God who calls you into His own kingdom and glory.

I THESSALONIANS 2:12 NASB

For we walk by faith, not by sight.

II CORINTHIANS 5:7 CSB

"Take My yoke upon you, and learn of Me; for I am meek and lowly in heart: and ye shall find rest unto your souls. For My yoke is easy, and My burden is light."

MATTHEW 11:29–30 KJV

"Whoever is not willing to carry the cross
and follow Me is not worthy of Me.
Those who try to hold on to their lives will give up true life.
Those who give up their lives for Me will hold on to true life."

MATTHEW 10:38–39 NCV

"Judge not, and you shall not be judged.
Condemn not, and you shall not be condemned.
Forgive, and you will be forgiven."

LUKE 6:37 NKJV

For those who seek to follow in Christ's footsteps, forgiveness isn't optional; it's a commandment. Jesus didn't say, "Forgive when you feel like it," or "Forgive when it's easy." He instructed His followers to forgive quickly, completely, and repeatedly: "Then Peter came to Him and said, 'Lord, how often shall my brother sin against me, and I forgive him? Up to seven times?' Jesus said to him, 'I do not say to you, up to seven times, but up to seventy times seven'" (Matthew 18:21–22 NKJV).

Christ's instructions to Peter also apply to each of us. We are commanded—not encouraged, not advised; we are commanded—to forgive and to keep forgiving, even when it's hard.

Bitterness will consume your life if you let it. Hatred will rob you of peace. The search for revenge will leave you frustrated. The only peace that lasts is God's peace, which is only available to those who make the choice to forgive. Sometimes forgiveness is a hard choice to make, but the rewards are always worth the sacrifice.

Forgiveness is the key
that unlocks the door of resentment
and the handcuffs of hatred.
It is a power that breaks
the chains of bitterness and
the shackles of selfishness.

CORRIE TEN BOOM

GOD'S PROMISES ABOUT FORGIVENESS

"But I say to you, love your enemies,
and pray for those who persecute you."
MATTHEW 5:44 NASB

*And be kind to one another,
tenderhearted, forgiving one another,
even as God in Christ forgave you.*
EPHESIANS 4:32 NKJV

"And whenever you stand praying,
if you have anything against anyone,
forgive him, so that your Father in heaven
will also forgive you your wrongdoing."
MARK 11:25 CSB

*"Blessed are the merciful,
for they will be shown mercy."*
MATTHEW 5:7 CSB

Friends and Friendship

A friend loves at all times,
and a brother is born for a time of adversity.
PROVERBS 17:17 NIV

Our friends are gifts from above. God places them along our path and asks us to treat them with kindness, love, and respect. His Word teaches us that true friendship is both a blessing and a treasure.

Emily Dickinson spoke for friends everywhere when she observed, "My friends are my estate." Dickinson understood that friends are among our most treasured possessions. But unlike a bank account or a stock certificate, the value of a true friendship is beyond measure.

Today, celebrate the joys of building and preserving your personal estate of lifelong friends. Give thanks for the laughter, the loyalty, the sharing, and the trust. And while you're at it, take the time to reconnect with a long-lost friend. When you do, you will have increased two personal fortunes at once.

You can't live the Christian life without a band of Christian friends, without a family of believers in which you find a place.
TIMOTHY KELLER

GOD'S PROMISES ABOUT FRIENDS AND FRIENDSHIP

As iron sharpens iron,
so people can improve each other.
PROVERBS 27:17 NCV

Oil and incense bring
joy to the heart,
and the sweetness of a friend
is better than self-counsel.
PROVERBS 27:9 CSB

It is good and pleasant when God's people
live together in peace!
PSALM 133:1 NCV

Dear friends,
if God loved us in this way,
we also must love one another.
1 JOHN 4:11 CSB

Thine own friend,
and thy father's friend,
forsake not.
PROVERBS 27:10 KJV

Gifts

Do not neglect the gift that is in you.

I TIMOTHY 4:14 NKJV

God gives each of us special talents and opportunities. And He bestows these gifts for a reason: so that we might use them for His glory. But the world tempts us to do otherwise. Here in the twenty-first century, life is filled to the brim with distractions and temptations, each of which has the potential to distance us from the path God intends for us to take.

Do you possess financial resources? Share them. Do you have a spiritual gift? Share it. Do you have a personal testimony about the things that Christ has done for you? Tell your story. Do you possess a particular talent? Hone that skill and use it for God's glory.

All your talents, all your opportunities, and all your gifts are on temporary loan from the Creator. Use those gifts while you can because time is short and the needs are great. In every undertaking, make God your partner. Then, just as He promised, God will bless you now and forever.

We are each given different gifts and talents by our Master. The thing that matters most is how we use what we have been given, not how much we make or do compared to someone else. What matters is that we spend ourselves.

FRANCIS CHAN

GOD'S PROMISES ABOUT GIFTS

God has given each of you a gift
from His great variety of spiritual gifts.
Use them well to serve one another.

I PETER 4:10 NLT

Now there are diversities of gifts,
but the same Spirit.

I CORINTHIANS 12:4 KJV

Every good and perfect gift is from above,
coming down from the Father of the heavenly lights,
who does not change like shifting shadows.

JAMES 1:17 NIV

"His master replied,
'Well done, good and faithful
servant! You have been faithful with a few
things; I will put you in charge of many things.
Come and share your master's happiness!'"

MATTHEW 25:21 NIV

I remind you to fan into flame the gift of God.

II TIMOTHY 1:6 NIV

You shall have no other gods before Me.

EXODUS 20:3 NKJV

For most of us, these are very busy times. We have obligations at home, at work, at school, or on social media. From the moment we rise until we drift off to sleep at night, we have things to do and people to contact. So, how do we find time for God? We must make time for Him, plain and simple. When we put God first, we're blessed. But when we succumb to the pressures and temptations of the world, we inevitably pay a price for our misguided priorities.

In the book of Exodus, God warns that we should put no gods before Him. Yet all too often, we place our Lord in second, third, or fourth place as we focus on other things. When we place our desires for possessions and status above our love for God—or when we yield to the countless distractions that surround us—we forfeit the peace that might otherwise be ours.

In the wilderness, Satan offered Jesus earthly power and unimaginable riches, but Jesus refused. Instead, He chose to worship His heavenly Father. We must do likewise by putting God first and worshiping Him only. God must come first. Always first.

The most

important thing

you must decide to do

every day is

put the Lord first.

ELIZABETH GEORGE

GOD'S PROMISES ABOUT PUTTING HIM FIRST

Therefore, whether you
eat or drink, or whatever you do,
do all to the glory of God.
I CORINTHIANS 10:31 NKJV

For this is the love of God,
that we keep His commandments.
And His commandments are not burdensome.
I JOHN 5:3 NKJV

How happy is everyone who fears the LORD,
who walks in His ways!
PSALM 128:1 CSB

But prove yourselves doers of the word,
and not merely hearers who delude themselves.
JAMES 1:22 NASB1995

We love Him,
because He first loved us.
I JOHN 4:19 KJV

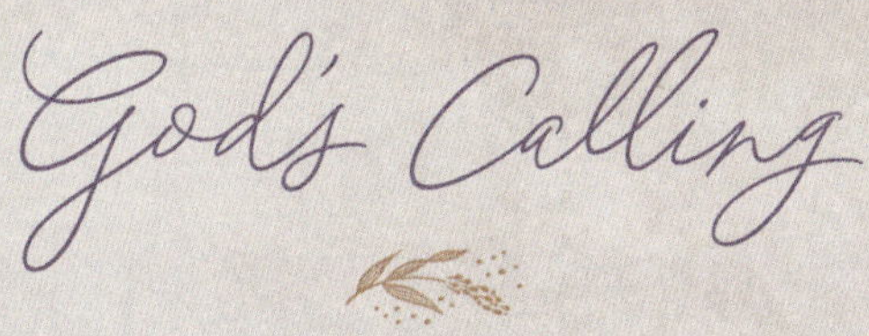

I urge you to live a life
worthy of the calling you have received.

EPHESIANS 4:1 NIV

God created you on purpose. He has a plan for your life that only you, with your unique array of talents and your own particular set of circumstances, can fulfill. The Lord is calling you; He's gently guiding you to the place where you can accomplish the greatest good for yourself and for His kingdom.

Have you already heard God's call? And are you doing your best to pursue His plan for your life? If so, you're blessed. But if you have not yet discovered God's plan for your life, don't panic. There's still time to hear His call and follow His path. To find that path, keep searching and keep praying. Answers will come—your Creator has placed you in a particular location, amid particular people, with unique opportunities to serve. And He has given you all the tools you need to accomplish His plans. So listen for His voice, watch for His signs, and prepare yourself for the call—His call—that is certain to come.

Only God's chosen task for you will ultimately satisfy. Do not wait until it is too late to realize the privilege of serving Him in His chosen position for you.

BETH MOORE

GOD'S PROMISES ABOUT HIS CALLING

But as God has distributed to each one,
as the Lord has called each one, so let him walk.

I CORINTHIANS 7:17 NKJV

And we know that all things work together for good to those who love God, to those who are the called according to His purpose.

ROMANS 8:28 NKJV

"For whoever does the will of God is My brother and My sister and mother."

MARK 3:35 NKJV

"For many are called, but few are chosen."

MATTHEW 22:14 KJV

For you have need of endurance,
so that when you have done the will of God,
you may receive what was promised.

HEBREWS 10:36 NASB

God's Forgiveness

If we confess our sins, He is faithful
and righteous to forgive us our sins
and to cleanse us from all unrighteousness.

1 JOHN 1:9 NASB1995

The Bible promises us that God will forgive our sins if we ask Him. It's our duty to ask. When we've fulfilled that responsibility, He will always keep His promise. Yet many of us continue to punish ourselves—with needless guilt and self-loathing—for mistakes that our Creator has long since forgiven and forgotten (Isaiah 43:25).

If you haven't managed to forgive yourself for some past mistake, or for a series of poor decisions, it's time to rearrange your thinking. If God has forgiven you, how can you withhold forgiveness from yourself? The answer, of course, is that God's mercy is intended to wash your sins away. That's what the Lord wants, and if you're good enough for Him, you're good enough.

Forgiveness doesn't make the situation okay,
it makes you okay.

BETH MOORE

GOD'S PROMISES ABOUT HIS FORGIVENESS

All the prophets testify about Him
that through His name everyone
who believes in Him receives forgiveness of sins.

ACTS 10:43 CSB

*Let us, then, feel very sure that we can come
before God's throne where there is grace.
There we can receive mercy and
grace to help us when we need it.*

HEBREWS 4:16 NCV

But the mercy of the LORD is from
everlasting to everlasting
upon them that fear Him,
and His righteousness unto
children's children.

PSALM 103:17 KJV

"Be merciful, just as your Father is merciful."

LUKE 6:36 NIV

"I am the one, I sweep away your transgressions for My own
sake and remember your sins no more."

ISAIAH 43:25 CSB

God's Guidance

Trust in the LORD with all your heart,
and lean not on your own understanding;
in all your ways acknowledge Him,
and He shall direct your paths.

PROVERBS 3:5–6 NKJV

When we ask for God's guidance, with our hearts and minds open to His direction, He will lead us along a path of His choosing. But for many of us, listening to God is hard. We have so many things we want, and so many needs to pray for, that we spend far more time talking at God than we do listening to Him.

Corrie ten Boom observed, "God's guidance is even more important than common sense. . . . I can declare that the deepest darkness is outshone by the light of Jesus." These words remind us that life is best lived when we seek the Lord's direction early and often.

Our Father has many ways to make Himself known. Our challenge is to make ourselves open to His instruction. So, if you're unsure of your next step, trust God's promises and talk to Him often. When you do, He'll guide your steps today, tomorrow, and forever.

God's guidance

is even more important

than common sense. . . .

I can declare that

the deepest darkness

is outshone by the light of Jesus.

CORRIE TEN BOOM

GOD'S PROMISES ABOUT HIS GUIDENCE

Yet LORD, You are our Father;
we are the clay, and You are our potter;
we all are the work of Your hands.

ISAIAH 64:8 CSB

***The LORD says, "I will guide you
along the best pathway for your life.
I will advise you and watch over you."***

PSALM 32:8 NLT

Teach me to do Your will, for You are my God;
Your Spirit is good. Lead me in the land of uprightness.

PSALM 143:10 NKJV

***Shew me Thy ways, O LORD;
teach me Thy paths. Lead me in Thy truth,
and teach me: for Thou art the God of my
salvation; on Thee do I wait all the day.***

PSALM 25:4–5 KJV

Morning by morning He wakens me and
opens my understanding to His will.
The Sovereign Lord has spoken to me, and I have listened.

ISAIAH 50:4–5 NLT

God's Love

And we have known and believed
the love that God has for us.
God is love, and he who abides
in love abides in God, and God in him.

I JOHN 4:16 NKJV

God's love is infinite. His love spans the entirety of His creation. His love touches the far reaches of His vast universe as well as the quiet corners of every human heart.

Sometimes, amid the crush of everyday life, God may seem very far away. He is not. God is always with us, night and day; He never leaves us, even for a moment. When we earnestly seek Him, we will find Him because He is always right here, waiting patiently for us to reach out to Him. Our job, of course, is to reach out to Him.

Nothing can separate you
from God's love, absolutely nothing.
God is enough for time,
God is enough for eternity.
God is enough!

HANNAH WHITALL SMITH

GOD'S PROMISES ABOUT HIS LOVE

We love Him,
because He first loved us.
I JOHN 4:19 KJV

This is how God showed His love among us:
He sent His one and only Son into the world
that we might live through Him.
I JOHN 4:9 NIV

Neither death nor life, neither angels nor demons,
neither the present nor the future, nor any powers,
neither height nor depth, nor anything else in all creation,
will be able to separate us from the love of God
that is in Christ Jesus our Lord.
ROMANS 8:38-39 NIV

Your love, Lord, reaches to the heavens,
Your faithfulness to the skies.
PSALM 36:5 NIV

Because of the Lord's great love we are not consumed,
for His compassions never fail.
They are new every morning; great is Your faithfulness.
LAMENTATIONS 3:22-23 NIV

God's Plan

But as it is written, what no eye has seen,
no ear has heard, and no human heart has conceived—
God has prepared these things for those who love Him.

I CORINTHIANS 2:9 CSB

God has a plan for this world and for your world. It's a plan that He understands perfectly, a plan that can bring you untold joy now and throughout eternity. But the Lord won't force His plan upon you. He's given you free will, the ability to make choices on your own. The totality of those choices will determine how well you fulfill God's calling.

Sometimes God makes Himself known in obvious ways, but more often His guidance is subtle. So we must be quiet to hear His voice.

If you're serious about discovering God's plan for your life—or rediscovering it—start spending quiet time with Him every day. Ask Him for direction. Pray for clarity. And be watchful for His signs. The more time you spend with Him, the sooner the answers will come.

Often God has to shut a door in our face so that He can subsequently open the door through which He wants us to go.

CATHERINE MARSHALL

GOD'S PROMISES ABOUT HIS PLAN

"For My thoughts are not your thoughts,
and your ways are not My ways....
For as heaven is higher than earth,
so My ways are higher than your ways,
and My thoughts than your thoughts."

ISAIAH 55:8–9 CSB

***And yet, O LORD, You are our Father.
We are the clay, and You are the potter.
We are all formed by Your hand.***

ISAIAH 64:8 NLT

"For whoever does the will of God
is My brother and My sister and mother."

MARK 3:35 NKJV

***It is God who is at work in you,
both to will and to work for His good pleasure.***

PHILIPPIANS 2:13 NASB1995

"We must do the works of Him
who sent Me while it is day.
Night is coming when no one can work."

JOHN 9:4 CSB

God's Presence

For the eyes of the LORD roam throughout the earth
to show Himself strong for those who
are wholeheartedly devoted to Him.

II CHRONICLES 16:9 CSB

God is everywhere: everywhere you've ever been, everywhere you'll ever be. He is not absent from our world, nor is He absent from your world. God is not "out there"; He is "right here," continuously reshaping His universe and continuously reshaping the lives of those who dwell in it.

Your Creator is with you always, listening to your thoughts and prayers, watching over your every move. If the demands of everyday life weigh down upon you, you may be tempted to ignore God's presence or—worse yet—lose faith in His promises. But when you quiet yourself and acknowledge His presence, God will touch your heart and renew your strength.

Psalm 46:10 remind us to "be still, and know that I am God" (NIV). When we do, we can be comforted in the knowledge that God does not love us from a distance. He is not just near. He is here.

To experience joy
on a daily basis,
learn what it means
to live in the moment . . .
Living in the moment helps us
recognize that God can
be found in this moment,
whether it contains joy or sorrow.

KAY WARREN

GOD'S PROMISES ABOUT HIS PRESENCE

"Be still, and know that I am God."

PSALM 46:10 KJV

Draw near to God,
and He will draw near to you.

JAMES 4:8 CSB

I know the LORD is
always with me.
I will not be shaken,
for He is right beside me.

PSALM 16:8 NLT

Though I walk through
the valley of the shadow
of death, I will fear no evil:
for Thou art with me.

PSALM 23:4 KJV

"I am not alone,
because the Father is with Me."

JOHN 16:32 NKJV

God's Promises

Let us hold on to the confession of our hope without wavering, since He who promised is faithful.

HEBREWS 10:23 CSB

The Bible contains promises upon which you, as a believer, can depend. When the Creator of the universe makes a pledge to you, He will keep it. No exceptions.

You can think of the Bible as a written contract between you and your heavenly Father. When you fulfill your obligations to Him, the Lord will most certainly fulfill His covenant to you.

When we accept Christ into our hearts, God promises us the opportunity to experience contentment, peace, and spiritual abundance. But more importantly, God promises that the priceless gift of eternal life will be ours. These promises should give us comfort. With God on our side, we have absolutely *nothing* to fear in this world and *everything* to hope for in the next.

Gather the riches of God's promises. Nobody can take away from you those texts from the Bible which you have learned by heart.

CORRIE TEN BOOM

GOD'S PROMISES

Sustain me as You promised,
and I will live; do not let me be
ashamed of my hope.
PSALM 119:116 CSB

As for God, His way is perfect:
the word of the LORD is tried:
He is a buckler to all those
that trust in Him.
PSALM 18:30 KJV

They will bind themselves to the LORD
with an eternal covenant
that will never again be forgotten.
JEREMIAH 50:5 NLT

My God is my rock,
in whom I take refuge,
my shield and the horn
of my salvation.
II SAMUEL 22:2–3 NIV

He heeded their prayer,
because they put their trust in Him.
I CHRONICLES 5:20 NKJV

God's Support

Nevertheless God, who comforts
the downcast, comforted us.

II CORINTHIANS 7:6 NKJV

God's Word promises that He will support you in good times and comfort you in hard times. The Creator of the universe stands ready to give you the strength to meet any challenge and the courage to face any adversity. When you ask for God's help, He responds in His own way and at His own appointed hour. But make no mistake: He always responds.

In a world brimming with dangers and temptations, God is the ultimate armor. In a world saturated with misleading messages, God's Word is the ultimate truth. In a world filled with frustrations and distractions, God's Son offers the ultimate peace.

Today, as you encounter the inevitable challenges of everyday life, remember that your heavenly Father never leaves you, not even for a moment. He's always available, always ready to listen, always ready to lead. When you make a habit of talking to Him early and often, He'll guide you and comfort you every day of your life.

God's all-sufficiency is a major.

Your inability is a minor.

Major in majors,

not in minors.

CORRIE TEN BOOM

GOD'S PROMISES ABOUT HIS SUPPORT

"My grace is sufficient for you,
for My power is made perfect in weakness."

II CORINTHIANS 12:9 NIV

*Therefore, we may boldly say:
The Lord is my helper; I will not be afraid.
What can man do to me?*

HEBREWS 13:6 CSB

Therefore humble yourselves under
the mighty hand of God, that He may exalt you in due time,
casting all your care upon Him, for He cares for you.

I PETER 5:6–7 NKJV

*The LORD is my light and my salvation—
whom should I fear? The LORD is the stronghold
of my life—whom should I dread?*

PSALM 27:1 CSB

The LORD is my shepherd; I shall not want.
He makes me to lie down in green pastures;
He leads me beside the still waters.
He restores my soul.

PSALM 23:1–3 NKJV

Grace

But because of His great love for us,
God, who is rich in mercy, made us alive
with Christ even when we were dead in transgressions—
it is by grace you have been saved.

EPHESIANS 2:4–5 NIV

God's grace is sufficient to meet our every need. No matter our circumstances, no matter our personal histories, the Lord's precious gifts are always available. All we need do is form a personal, life-altering relationship with His only begotten Son, and we're secure, now and forever.

Grace is unearned, undeserved favor from God. His grace is available to each of us. No sin is too terrible, no behavior too outrageous, to separate us from God's love. We are saved by grace *through faith*. Jesus paid for our sins on the cross, and when we trust Him completely, God pronounces us "not guilty" of our transgressions.

Have you accepted Christ as your King, your Shepherd, and your Savior? If so, you are protected now and forever. If not, this moment is the appropriate time to trust God's Son and accept God's grace. It's never too soon, or too late, to welcome Jesus into your heart.

How beautiful it is
to learn that grace
isn't fragile,
and that in the family of God
we can fail and not be a failure.

GLORIA GAITHER

GOD'S PROMISES ABOUT GRACE

But grow in the grace and knowledge
of our Lord and Savior Jesus Christ.
To Him be the glory, both now and to the day of eternity.

II PETER 3:18 NASB

In Him we have redemption through His blood, the forgiveness of our trespasses, according to the riches of His grace that He richly poured out on us with all wisdom and understanding.

EPHESIANS 1:7–8 CSB

"My grace is sufficient for you,
for My power is made perfect in weakness."

II CORINTHIANS 12:9 NIV

But God gives us even more grace, as the Scripture says, "God is against the proud, but He gives grace to the humble."

JAMES 4:6 NCV

For by grace you have been saved through faith,
and that not of yourselves; it is the gift of God,
not of works, lest anyone should boast.

EPHESIANS 2:8–9 NKJV

Happiness

Those who listen to instruction will prosper;
those who trust the LORD will be joyful.

PROVERBS 16:20 NLT

Everywhere we turn, or so it seems, the message is clear: happiness is for sale, and if we have enough money, we can buy it. But God's Word contains a different message. In the Bible, we are taught that happiness is a by-product, the result of living in harmony with God's plan for our lives. Obedience is the path to peace, love, and happiness. Disobedience is the path to discouragement, dissatisfaction, and doubt.

Happiness also depends on the way we think. If we form the habit of focusing on the positive aspects of life, we tend to be happier. But if we choose to dwell on the negatives, our very own thoughts have the power to make us miserable.

Do you want to be a happy Christian? Then you must start by being an obedient Christian. Then you must set your mind and heart upon God's blessings. When you think about it, you have many reasons to be joyful. When you count your blessings every day—and obey your Creator—you'll discover that happiness is not a commodity to be purchased; it is, instead, the natural consequence of walking daily with God.

When we bring sunshine

into the lives of others,

we're warmed by it ourselves.

When we spill a little happiness,

it splashes on us.

BARBARA JOHNSON

GOD'S PROMISES ABOUT HAPPINESS

If they obey and serve Him,
they will spend the rest of
their days in prosperity
and their years in contentment.

JOB 36:11 NIV

***"I have come that they may have life,
and that they may have it more abundantly."***

JOHN 10:10 NKJV

Happiness makes a person smile,
but sadness can break a person's spirit.

PROVERBS 15:13 NCV

***A joyful heart is good medicine,
but a broken spirit
dries up the bones.***

PROVERBS 17:22 CSB

Joyful is the person who
finds wisdom, the one who
gains understanding.

PROVERBS 3:13 NLT

Helping Others

Carry one another's burdens;
in this way you will fulfill the law of Christ.

GALATIANS 6:2 CSB

If you're looking for somebody to help, you won't have to look very far. Somebody very close needs a helping hand, or a hot meal, or a pat on the back, or a prayer. In order to find that person, you'll need to keep your eyes and your heart open, and you'll need to stay focused on the needs of others. Focusing, however, is not as simple as it seems.

We live in a fast-paced, media-driven world filled with countless temptations and time-wasting distractions. Sometimes we may convince ourselves that we simply don't have the time or the resources to offer help to the needy. Such thoughts are misguided. Caring for our neighbors must be *our* priority because it is *God's* priority.

God has a specific plan for your life, and part of that plan involves service to His children. Service is not a burden; it's an opportunity. Seize your opportunity today. Tomorrow may be too late.

It is one of the most beautiful compensations of life, that no man can sincerely try to help another without helping himself.

RALPH WALDO EMERSON

GOD'S PROMISES ABOUT HELPING OTHERS

Let us not become weary in doing good,
for at the proper time we will reap
a harvest if we do not give up.
GALATIANS 6:9 NIV

Whenever you are able,
do good to people
who need help.
PROVERBS 3:27 NCV

If you have two shirts, give one to the poor.
If you have food, share it with those who are hungry.
LUKE 3:11 NLT

"And the King will answer them,
'Truly I tell you, whatever you did
for one of the least of these brothers and sisters
of Mine, you did for Me.'"
MATTHEW 25:40 CSB

Therefore, as we have opportunity,
let us work for the good of all,
especially for those
who belong to the household of faith.
GALATIANS 6:10 CSB

Let us hold fast the confession of our hope
without wavering, for He who promised is faithful.

HEBREWS 10:23 NASB1995

God's promises give us hope: hope for today, hope for tomorrow, hope for all eternity. The hope that the world offers is temporary, at best. But the hope that God offers never grows old and never goes out of date. It's no wonder, then, that when we pin our hopes on worldly resources, we are often disappointed. Thankfully, God has no such record of failure.

The Bible teaches that the Lord blesses those who trust in His wisdom and follow in the footsteps of His Son. Will you count yourself among that number? When you do, you'll have every reason on earth—and in heaven—to be hopeful about your future. After all, God has made important promises to you, promises that He is certainly going to keep. So be hopeful, be optimistic, be faithful, and do your best. Then, leave the rest up to God. Your destiny is safe with Him.

Never yield to gloomy anticipation.
Place your hope and confidence in God.
He has no record of failure.

LETTIE COWMAN

GOD'S PROMISES ABOUT HOPE

This hope we have as an anchor of the soul,
a hope both sure and steadfast.

HEBREWS 6:19 NASB1995

I say to myself,
"The LORD is mine, so I hope in Him."

LAMENTATIONS 3:24 NCV

The LORD is good to those who wait for Him,
to the soul who seeks Him.
It is good that one should hope
and wait quietly for the salvation of the LORD.

LAMENTATIONS 3:25–26 NKJV

Hope deferred makes
the heart sick,
But when the desire comes,
it is a tree of life.

PROVERBS 13:12 NKJV

Be strong and courageous,
all you who put your hope in the LORD.

PSALM 31:24 CSB

Joy

This is the day which the LORD has made;
let us rejoice and be glad in it.
PSALM 118:24 NASB1995

The joy that the world offers is fleeting and incomplete: here today, gone tomorrow, not coming back anytime soon. But God's joy is different. His joy has staying power. In fact, it's a gift that never stops giving to those who welcome His Son into their hearts.

Psalm 100 reminds us to celebrate the lives that God has given us: "Shout for joy to the LORD, all the earth. Worship the LORD with gladness; come before Him with joyful songs" (v. 1–2 NIV). Yet sometimes, amid the inevitable complications and predicaments that are woven into the fabric of everyday life, we forget to rejoice. Instead of celebrating life, we complain about it. This is an understandable mistake, but a mistake nonetheless. As Christians, we are called by our Creator to live joyfully and abundantly. To do otherwise is to squander His spiritual gifts.

This day and every day, Christ offers you His peace and His joy. Accept it and share it with others, just as He has shared His joy with you.

Among the most joyful people I have known have been some who seem to have had no human reason for joy. The sweet fragrance of Christ has shown through their lives.

ELISABETH ELLIOT

GOD'S PROMISES ABOUT JOY

Rejoice in the Lord always.
Again I will say, rejoice!
PHILIPPIANS 4:4 NKJV

Rejoice always, pray without ceasing,
in everything give thanks;
for this is the will
of God in Christ Jesus for you.
I THESSALONIANS 5:16–18 NKJV

"I have told you these things so that My joy
may be in you and your joy may be complete."
JOHN 15:11 CSB

"Until now you have asked for nothing
in My name. Ask and you will receive,
so that your joy may be complete."
JOHN 16:24 CSB

"So you also have sorrow now.
But I will see you again.
Your hearts will rejoice,
and no one will take away your joy from you."
JOHN 16:22 CSB

Judging Others

"Judge not, and you shall not be judged.
Condemn not, and you shall not be condemned.
Forgive, and you will be forgiven."

LUKE 6:37 NKJV

The need to judge others seems to be woven into the very fabric of human consciousness. We mortals feel compelled to serve as informal judges and juries, pronouncing our own verdicts on the actions and perceived motivations of others, all the while excusing—or oftentimes hiding—our own shortcomings. But God's Word instructs us to let Him be the judge. He knows that we, with our limited knowledge and personal biases, are simply ill-equipped to assess the actions of others. The act of judging, then, becomes not only an act of futility, but also an affront to our Creator.

When Jesus came upon a woman who had been condemned by the Pharisees, He spoke not only to the people who had gathered there, but also to all generations. Christ warned, "He that is without sin among you, let him first cast a stone at her" (John 8:7 KJV). The message is clear: because we are all sinners, we must refrain from the temptation to judge others.

So the next time you're tempted to cast judgment on another human being, resist that temptation. God hasn't called you to be a judge; He's called you to be a witness.

Don't judge other people

more harshly

than you want

God to judge you.

MARIE T. FREEMAN

GOD'S PROMISES ABOUT JUDGING OTHERS

Don't criticize one another, brothers and sisters. Anyone who defames or judges a fellow believer defames and judges the law. If you judge the law, you are not a doer of the law but a judge.

JAMES 4:11 CSB

Therefore, every one of you who judges is without excuse. For when you judge another, you condemn yourself, since you, the judge, do the same things.

ROMANS 2:1 CSB

Do everything without
grumbling and arguing,
so that you may be blameless and pure.

PHILIPPIANS 2:14–15 CSB

Those who guard their lips
preserve their lives,
but those who speak rashly
will come to ruin.

PROVERBS 13:3 NIV

Kindness and Compassion

"Therefore, whatever you want
men to do to you, do also to them,
for this is the Law and the Prophets."

MATTHEW 7:12 NKJV

Jesus set the example: He was compassionate, loving, and kind. If we seek to follow Him, we, too, must combine compassionate hearts with willing hands.

John Wesley said: "Do all the good you can, by all the means you can, in all the ways you can, in all the places you can, at all the times you can, to all the people you can, as long as ever you can." His advice still applies. In order to follow in Christ's footsteps, we must be compassionate. There is simply no other way.

Never underestimate the power of kindness. You never know when a kind word or gesture might significantly improve someone's day, or week, or life. So be quick to offer words of encouragement, and smiles, and pats on the back. Be generous with your resources and your time. Make kindness the cornerstone of your dealings with others. They will be blessed, and you will be too. And everybody wins.

I would rather make mistakes

in kindness and compassion

than work miracles

in unkindness and hardness.

MOTHER TERESA

GOD'S PROMISES ABOUT KINDNESS AND COMPASSION

"A new commandment I give unto you,
that ye love one another; as I have loved you,
that ye also love one another."

JOHN 13:34 KJV

***Who among you is wise and understanding?
By his good conduct he should show
that his works are done in the
gentleness that comes from wisdom.***

JAMES 3:13 CSB

Be kind to one another, tender-hearted,
forgiving each other, just as God in Christ
also has forgiven you.

EPHESIANS 4:32 NASB1995

***And let us not grow weary while doing good,
for in due season we shall reap
if we do not lose heart.***

GALATIANS 6:9 NKJV

"And the King will answer and say to them,
'Assuredly, I say to you, inasmuch as you did it
to one of the least of these My brethren, you did it to Me.'"

MATTHEW 25:40 NKJV

Love

And now abide faith, hope, love, these three;
but the greatest of these is love.

I CORINTHIANS 13:13 NKJV

God is love, and He intends that we share His love with the world. But He won't force us to be loving and kind. He places that responsibility squarely on our shoulders.

Love, like everything else in this world, begins and ends with God, but the middle part belongs to us. The Creator gives each of us the opportunity to be kind, to be courteous, and to be loving. He gives each of us the chance to obey the Golden Rule, or to make up our own rules as we go. If we obey God's instructions, we're secure, but if we do otherwise, we suffer.

Christ's words are clear: "'Love the Lord your God with all your heart and with all your soul and with all your mind.' This is the first and greatest commandment. And the second is like it: 'Love your neighbor as yourself.' All the Law and the Prophets hang on these two commandments" (Matthew 22:37–40 NIV). We are commanded to love the One who first loved us and then to share His love with the world. And the next move is always ours.

The vast ocean of Love cannot be measured or explained, but it can be experienced.

SARAH YOUNG

GOD'S PROMISES ABOUT LOVE

"A new commandment I give unto you,
that ye love one another; as I have loved you,
that ye also love one another."

JOHN 13:34 KJV

Love is patient, love is kind.
Love does not envy,
is not boastful, is not arrogant.

I CORINTHIANS 13:4 CSB

Beloved, if God so loved us,
we ought also to love one another.

I JOHN 4:11 KJV

Above all,
love each other deeply,
because love covers a multitude of sins.

I PETER 4:8 NIV

And we have known and believed the love
that God has for us. God is love, and he
who abides in love abides in God, and God in him.

I JOHN 4:16 NKJV

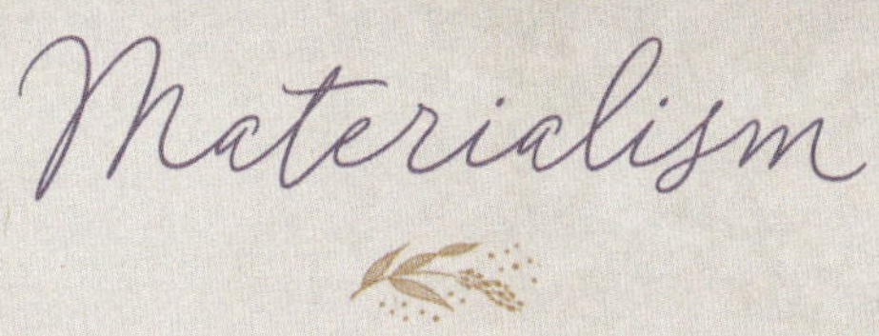

Materialism

"No one can serve two masters.
For you will hate one and love the other;
you will be devoted to one and despise the other.
You cannot serve God and be enslaved to money."

LUKE 16:13 NLT

The world's message is abundantly clear: collect enough material possessions and you'll be happy. But God's Word warns against such shallow thinking. The Bible teaches us that the love of money—and the love of things that money can buy—is a trap that inevitably leads to disappointment, to disillusionment, and, ultimately, to destruction.

On the grand stage of a well-lived life, material possessions should play a rather small role. Of course, we all need the basic necessities of life, but once we meet those needs for ourselves and for our families, the piling up of possessions creates more problems than it solves. Our real riches, of course, are not of this world. We are never really rich until we are rich in spirit.

So, if you're a woman who finds herself wrapped up in the concerns of the material world, it's time to reorder your priorities. And it's time to begin storing up riches that will endure throughout eternity—the spiritual kind.

It's sobering to contemplate how much time, effort, sacrifice, compromise, and attention we give to acquiring and increasing our supply of something that is totally insignificant in eternity.

ANNE GRAHAM LOTZ

GOD'S PROMISES ABOUT MATERIALISM

"For where your treasure is,
there your heart will be also."
LUKE 12:34 CSB

***Keep your life free from the love of money.
Be satisfied with what you have, for He Himself
has said, I will never leave you or abandon you.***
HEBREWS 13:5 CSB

We brought nothing into the world,
so we can take nothing out.
But, if we have food and clothes,
we will be satisfied with that.
I TIMOTHY 6:7–8 NCV

***Do not love the world or the things in the world.
If anyone loves the world,
love of the Father is not in him.***
I JOHN 2:15 CSB

There is one who makes himself rich,
yet has nothing; and one who makes
himself poor, yet has great riches.
PROVERBS 13:7 NKJV

Miracles

Is anything too hard for the LORD?

GENESIS 18:14 NKJV

God's power has no limitations. He is not restrained by the laws of nature because He created those laws. At any time, at any place, under any set of circumstances, He can accomplish anything He chooses. The things that seem miraculous to us are, to Him, expressions of His power and His love.

Do you expect God to work miracles in your own life? You should. From the moment He created our universe out of nothingness, the Lord has made a habit of doing miraculous things. And He's still working miracles today.

With God nothing is impossible. His wondrous works come in all shapes and sizes, so keep your eyes and your heart open. Somewhere, a miracle is about to happen, and it might just happen to *you*.

It is wonderful what miracles
God works in wills
that are utterly surrendered to Him.

HANNAH WHITALL SMITH

GOD'S PROMISES ABOUT MIRACLES

God confirmed the message by giving signs
and wonders and various miracles and
gifts of the Holy Spirit whenever He chose.

HEBREWS 2:4 NLT

What no eye has seen,
what no ear has heard, and what no human
mind has conceived—the things God has
prepared for those who love Him.

I CORINTHIANS 2:9 NIV

You are the God of great wonders!
You demonstrate Your awesome power
among the nations.

PSALM 77:14 NLT

And Jesus looking upon them saith,
"With men it is impossible, but not with God:
for with God all things are possible."

MARK 10:27 KJV

For with God nothing
shall be impossible.

LUKE 1:37 KJV

Obedience

Now by this we know that we know Him,
if we keep His commandments.

I JOHN 2:3 NKJV

God's instructions to mankind are contained in a book like no other: the Holy Bible. When we obey God's commandments and listen carefully to the conscience He has placed in our hearts, we are secure. But if we disobey our Creator, if we choose to ignore the teachings and the warnings of His Word, we do so at great peril.

Susanna Wesley said, "There are two things to do about the gospel: believe it and behave it." Her words serve as a powerful reminder that, as Christians, we are called to take God's promises seriously and to live in accordance with His teachings.

God gave us His commandments for a reason: so that we might obey them and be blessed. Yet we live in a world that presents us with countless temptations to stray far from His path. It is our responsibility to resist those temptations with vigor. Obedience isn't just the best way to experience the full measure of God's blessings; it's the only way.

When we are obedient,
God guides our steps and our stops.

CORRIE TEN BOOM

GOD'S PROMISES ABOUT OBEDIENCE

We must obey God rather than men.

ACTS 5:29 NASB

Teach me, O Lord, the way of Thy statutes,
and I shall observe it to the end.

PSALM 119:33 NASB1995

Trust in the Lord with all your heart,
and lean not on your own understanding;
in all your ways acknowledge Him,
and He shall direct your paths.

PROVERBS 3:5–6 NKJV

Praise the Lord!
Happy are those
who respect the Lord,
who want what He commands.

PSALM 112:1 NCV

But prove yourselves doers of the word,
and not merely hearers who delude themselves.

JAMES 1:22 NASB1995

Past

Do not remember the former things,
nor consider the things of old. Behold, I will do a new thing.

ISAIAH 43:18–19 NKJV

Since we can't change the pains and disappointments of the past, why do so many of us insist upon replaying them over and over again in our minds? Perhaps it's because we can't find it in our hearts to forgive the people who have hurt us. Being mere mortals, we seek revenge, not reconciliation, and we harbor hatred in our hearts, sometimes for decades.

Reinhold Niebuhr composed a simple verse that came to be known as the Serenity Prayer: "God, grant me the serenity to accept the things I cannot change, the courage to change the things I can, and the wisdom to know the difference." Obviously, we cannot change the past. It is what it was and forever will be. The present, of course, is a different matter.

Today is filled with opportunities to live, to love, to work, to play, and to celebrate life. If we sincerely wish to build a better tomorrow, we can start building it today, in the present moment. So, if you've endured a difficult past, accept it, learn from it, and forgive everybody, including yourself. Once you've made peace with your past, don't spend too much time there. Instead, live in the precious present, where opportunities abound and change is still possible.

We set our eyes on the finish line,

forgetting the past,

and straining toward

the mark of spiritual

maturity and fruitfulness.

VONETTE BRIGHT

GOD'S PROMISES ABOUT THE PAST

One thing I do, forgetting those things
which are behind and reaching forward
to those things which are ahead,
I press toward the goal for the prize
of the upward call of God in Christ Jesus.

PHILIPPIANS 3:13–14 NKJV

*Have mercy on me, O God, according to
Your unfailing love; according to Your great
compassion blot out my transgressions.
Wash away all my iniquity and
cleanse me from my sin.*

PSALM 51:1–2 NIV

Your old sinful self has died,
and your new life is
kept with Christ in God.

COLOSSIANS 3:3 NCV

*He restoreth my soul: He leadeth me in
the paths of righteousness for His name's sake.*

PSALM 23:3 KJV

A person's wisdom yields patience;
it is to one's glory to overlook an offense.

PROVERBS 19:11 NIV

Time and again, the Bible promises us that patience is its own reward, but not its only reward. Yet we human beings are, by nature, an impatient lot. We know what we want and we know when we want it: right now!

We live in an imperfect world inhabited by imperfect family members, imperfect friends, imperfect acquaintances, and imperfect strangers. Sometimes we inherit troubles from these imperfect people, and sometimes we create troubles for ourselves. In either case, what's required is patience: patience for other people's shortcomings as well as our own.

Proverbs 16:32 teaches, "Better to be patient than powerful; better to have self-control than to conquer a city" (NLT). But for most of us, waiting patiently is hard. We are fallible beings who want things today, not tomorrow. Still, God instructs us to be patient, and that's what we must do. It's the peaceful way to live.

The times we find ourselves having to wait on others may be the perfect opportunities to train ourselves to wait on the Lord.

JONI EARECKSON TADA

GOD'S PROMISES ABOUT PATIENCE

Patience of spirit is
better than haughtiness of spirit.
ECCLESIASTES 7:8 NASB1995

Better to be patient than powerful; better to have self-control than to conquer a city.
PROVERBS 16:32 NLT

But if we hope for what we
do not yet have,
we wait for it patiently.
ROMANS 8:25 NIV

Be joyful in hope,
patient in affliction,
faithful in prayer.
ROMANS 12:12 NIV

The LORD is good to those who depend on Him, to those who search for Him. So it is good to wait quietly for salvation from the LORD.
LAMENTATIONS 3:25–26 NLT

Peace

"Peace I leave with you, My peace I give to you;
not as the world gives do I give to you.
Let not your heart be troubled, neither let it be afraid."

JOHN 14:27 NKJV

Peace. It's such a beautiful word. It conveys images of serenity, contentment, and freedom from the trials and tribulations of everyday existence. Peace means freedom from conflict, freedom from inner turmoil, and freedom from worry. Peace is such a beautiful concept that advertisers and marketers attempt to sell it with images of relaxed vacationers lounging on the beach or happy senior citizens celebrating on the golf course. But contrary to the implied claims of modern media, real peace, genuine peace, isn't for sale. At any price.

Have you discovered the genuine peace that can be yours through Christ? Or are you still scurrying after the illusion of peace that the world promises but cannot deliver? If you've turned things over to Jesus, you'll be blessed now and forever. So what are you waiting for? Let Him rule your heart and your thoughts, beginning now. When you do, you'll experience the peace that only He can give.

Peace comes

in situations

completely surrendered

to the sovereign

authority of Christ.

BETH MOORE

GOD'S PROMISES ABOUT PEACE

He Himself is our peace.

EPHESIANS 2:14 NASB

The peace of God, which passeth all understanding, shall keep your hearts and minds through Christ Jesus.

PHILIPPIANS 4:7 KJV

But the fruit of the Spirit is love,
joy, peace, patience, kindness,
goodness, faithfulness, gentleness, self-control.
The law is not against such things.

GALATIANS 5:22–23 CSB

"I will give peace, real peace, to those far and near, and I will heal them," says the LORD.

ISAIAH 57:19 NCV

"These things I have spoken to you,
that in Me you may have peace.
In the world you will have tribulation;
but be of good cheer,
I have overcome the world."

JOHN 16:33 NKJV

Perseverance

Let us not become weary in doing good,
for at the proper time we will
reap a harvest if we do not give up.

GALATIANS 6:9 NIV

Occasionally, good things happen with little or no effort. Somebody wins the lottery, or inherits a fortune, or stumbles onto a financial bonanza by being at the right place at the right time. But more often than not, good things happen to people who work hard, and keep working hard, when just about everybody else has gone home or given up.

Christina Rossetti said, "Can anything be sadder than work left unfinished? Yes, work never begun." And St. Catherine of Siena observed, "Nothing great was ever done without much enduring." Both women were right. Perseverance pays.

Every marathon has a finish line, and so does yours. So keep putting one foot in front of the other, pray for strength, and don't give up. Whether you realize it or not, you're up to the challenge if you persevere. And with God's help, that's exactly what you'll do.

By perseverance the snail reached the ark.

CHARLES SPURGEON

GOD'S PROMISES ABOUT PERSEVERANCE

But as for you, be strong; don't give up,
for your work has a reward.

II CHRONICLES 15:7 CSB

*We are hard-pressed on
every side, yet not crushed;
we are perplexed, but not in despair.*

II CORINTHIANS 4:8 NKJV

Finishing is better than starting.
Patience is better than pride.

ECCLESIASTES 7:8 NLT

*For you have need of endurance,
so that when you have done the will of God,
you may receive what was promised.*

HEBREWS 10:36 NASB

So let us run the race that is before us
and never give up. We should remove from
our lives anything that would get in the way
and the sin that so easily holds us back.

HEBREWS 12:1 NCV

Praise

Let everything that breathes praise the LORD. Hallelujah!

PSALM 150:6 CSB

Time and again, God's Word teaches that it pays to praise our Creator. God doesn't need our praise, nor does He require it before He dispenses His blessings. But we need the experience of praising Him, and He smiles upon us when we do.

When we consider God's blessings and the sacrifices of His Son, just how thankful should we be? Should we praise our Creator once a day? Are two prayers enough? Is it sufficient that we praise our heavenly Father at mealtimes and bedtimes? The answer, of course, is no. When we consider how richly we have been blessed, now and forever—and when we consider the price Christ paid on the cross—it becomes clear that we should offer many prayers of thanks throughout the day.

Our lives expand or contract in proportion to our gratitude. When we are appropriately grateful for God's countless blessings, we experience His peace. But if we ignore His gifts, we invite stress, anxiety, and sadness into our lives. So, throughout this day, pause and say silent prayers of thanks. When you do, you'll discover that a grateful heart reaps countless blessings that a hardened heart will never know.

This is my story,

this is my song,

praising my Savior,

all the day long.

FANNY CROSBY

GOD'S PROMISES ABOUT PRAISE

Great is the Lord!
He is most worthy of praise!
No one can measure His greatness.

PSALM 145:3 NLT

***In everything give thanks;
for this is the will of God in Christ Jesus for you.***

I THESSALONIANS 5:18 NKJV

At the name of Jesus every knee should bow,
of things in heaven, and things in earth, and things under
the earth; and that every tongue should confess
that Jesus Christ is Lord, to the glory of God the Father.

PHILIPPIANS 2:10–11 KJV

***The Lord is my
strength and my song;
He has become my salvation.***

EXODUS 15:2 CSB

From the rising of the sun to its setting,
the name of the Lord is to be praised.

PSALM 113:3 NASB

Rejoice always, pray without ceasing,
in everything give thanks; for this is the
will of God in Christ Jesus for you.

I THESSALONIANS 5:16–18 NKJV

Prayer is a powerful tool that you can use to change your world and change yourself. God hears every prayer and responds in His own way and according to His own timetable. When you make a habit of consulting Him about everything, He'll guide you along a path of His choosing, which, by the way, is the path you should take. And when you petition Him for strength, He'll give you the courage to face any problem and the power to meet any challenge.

So today, instead of turning things over in your mind, turn them over to God in prayer. Take your concerns to the Lord and leave them there. Your heavenly Father is listening, and He wants to hear from you. Now.

Don't pray when you feel like it.
Have an appointment
with the Lord and keep it.

CORRIE TEN BOOM

GOD'S PROMISES ABOUT PRAYER

I desire therefore that the men pray everywhere,
lifting up holy hands, without wrath and doubting.

I TIMOTHY 2:8 NKJV

Is anyone among you suffering?
He should pray.

JAMES 5:13 CSB

Confess your trespasses to one another,
and pray for one another, that you may be healed.
The effective, fervent prayer of a righteous man avails much.

JAMES 5:16 NKJV

"And whenever you stand praying,
if you have anything against anyone,
forgive him, so that your Father in heaven
will also forgive you your wrongdoing."

MARK 11:25 CSB

"Ask, and it will be given to you; seek, and you will find;
knock, and it will be opened to you.
For everyone who asks receives, and he who seeks finds,
and to him who knocks it will be opened."

MATTHEW 7:7–8 NASB1995

In Him we have also received an inheritance, because we were predestined according to the plan of the One who works out everything in agreement with the purpose of His will.

EPHESIANS 1:11 CSB

God doesn't do things by accident. He didn't put you here by chance. The Lord didn't deliver you to your particular place, at this particular time, with your particular set of talents and opportunities on a whim. He has a plan, a one-of-a-kind mission designed especially for you. Discovering that plan may take time. But if you keep asking God for guidance, He'll lead you along a path of His choosing and give you every tool you need to fulfill His will.

Of course, you'll probably encounter a few impediments as you attempt to discover the exact nature of God's purpose for your life. And you may travel down a few dead ends along the way. But if you keep searching, and if you genuinely seek the Lord's guidance, He'll reveal His plans at a time and place of His own choosing.

Today and every day, God is beckoning you to hear His voice and follow His plan for your life. When you listen—and when you answer His call—you'll be amazed at the wonderful things that an all-knowing, all-powerful God can do.

When God gives

you a mission,

He also gives

you everything

you need to fulfill

that mission.

ELIZABETH GEORGE

GOD'S PROMISES ABOUT PURPOSE

So whether you eat or drink,
or whatever you do,
do it all for the glory of God.

I CORINTHIANS 10:31 NLT

For we are God's coworkers.
You are God's field,
God's building.

I CORINTHIANS 3:9 CSB

For we are His workmanship,
created in Christ Jesus for good works,
which God prepared ahead of time for us to do.

EPHESIANS 2:10 CSB

"We must do the works
of Him who sent Me while
it is day. Night is coming
when no one can work."

JOHN 9:4 CSB

And whatever you do, do it heartily,
as to the Lord and not to men.

COLOSSIANS 3:23 NKJV

Quiet Time

Now in the morning,
having risen a long while before daylight,
He went out and departed to a solitary place;
and there He prayed.

MARK 1:35 NKJV

Jesus understood the importance of silence. He spent precious hours alone with God, and so should we. But with our busy schedules, we're tempted to rush from place to place, checking smart phones along the way, leaving no time to contemplate spiritual matters.

You live in a noisy world, a complicated society where sights and sounds surround you and silence is in short supply. Everywhere you turn, or so it seems, the media seeks to grab your attention and hijack your thoughts. You're surrounded by big screens and little ones. And your phone can keep you logged in day and night if you let it. Don't let it.

Today and every day, you need quiet, uninterrupted time alone with God. You need to be still and listen for His voice. And you need to seek His guidance in matters great and small. Your Creator has important plans for your day and your life. And He's trying to get His message through. You owe it to Him—and to yourself—to listen and to learn *in silence*.

A little quiet reflection
will remind me that
yes to God always leads
in the end to joy.

ELISABETH ELLIOT

GOD'S PROMISES ABOUT QUIET TIME

Truly my soul silently waits for God;
from Him comes my salvation.
PSALM 62:1 NKJV

Be still, and know
that I am God.
PSALM 46:10 KJV

"Listen in silence before Me."
ISAIAH 41:1 NLT

In quietness and in confidence
shall be your strength.
ISAIAH 30:15 KJV

To everything
there is a season...
a time to keep silence,
and a time to speak.
ECCLESIASTES 3:1, 7 KJV

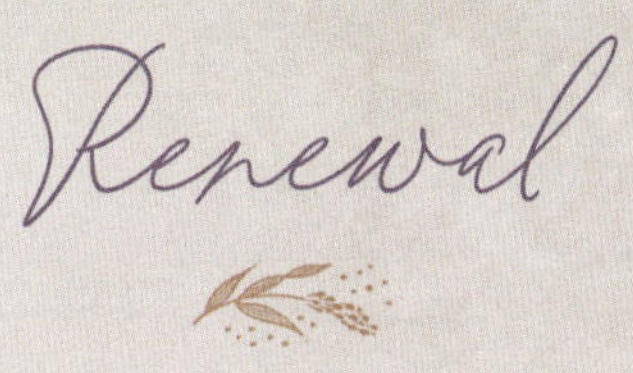

Therefore, if anyone is in Christ,
he is a new creation; old things have passed away;
behold, all things have become new.
II CORINTHIANS 5:17 NKJV

For busy citizens of the twenty-first century, it's easy to become overcommitted, overworked, and over-stressed. If we choose, we can be connected 24-7, sparing just enough time for a few hours' sleep each night. What we need is time to renew and recharge, but where can we find the time? We can—and should—find it with God.

God can renew your strength and restore your spirit if you let Him. But He won't force you to slow down, and He won't insist that you get enough sleep at night. He leaves those choices up to you.

If you're feeling chronically tired or discouraged, it's time to rearrange your schedule, turn off the TV, power down the phone, and spend quiet time with your Creator. He knows what you need, and He wants you to experience His peace and His love. He's ready, willing, and perfectly able to renew your strength and help you prioritize the items on your to-do list if you ask Him. In fact, He's ready to hear your prayers right now. Please don't make Him wait.

The creation of a new heart,
the renewing of a right spirit
is an omnipotent work of God.
Leave it to the Creator.

HENRY DRUMMOND

GOD'S PROMISES ABOUT RENEWAL

Instead, let the Spirit renew
your thoughts and attitudes.
Put on your new nature,
created to be like God—
truly righteous and holy.

EPHESIANS 4:23–24 NLT

Those who hope in the LORD will renew their strength. They will soar on wings like eagles; they will run and not grow weary, they will walk and not be faint.

ISAIAH 40:31 NIV

"Remember ye not the
former things, neither consider
the things of old.
Behold, I will do a new thing."

ISAIAH 43:18–19 KJV

Finally, brothers and sisters, rejoice. Become mature, be encouraged, be of the same mind, be at peace, and the God of love and peace will be with you.

II CORINTHIANS 13:11 CSB

Service and Serving God

"The greatest among you will be your servant.
For those who exalt themselves will be humbled,
and those who humble themselves will be exalted."

MATTHEW 23:11–12 NIV

How do we achieve greatness in the eyes of God? By accumulating wealth? By acquiring power? By gaining fame, popularity, or prestige? Of course not. We achieve greatness in God's eyes by serving His children gladly, humbly, and often.

Everywhere we look, the needs are great. Whether here at home or halfway around the globe, so many people are enduring difficult circumstances. They need help, and as Christians, we are instructed to serve them.

Jesus came to this world, not to conquer but to serve. We must do likewise by helping those who cannot help themselves. When we do, our lives will be blessed by the One who first served us.

What is needed for happy effectual service
is simply to put your work
into the Lord's hand, and leave it there.

HANNAH WHITALL SMITH

GOD'S PROMISES ABOUT SERVING HIM

Shepherd God's flock, for whom you
are responsible. Watch over them because you want to,
not because you are forced. That is how God wants it.
Do it because you are happy to serve.

I PETER 5:2 NCV

As each one has received a gift,
minister it to one another,
as good stewards
of the manifold grace of God.

I PETER 4:10 NKJV

"Blessed are those servants, whom the lord
when he cometh shall find watching."

LUKE 12:37 KJV

"And the King will answer and say to them,
'Assuredly, I say to you, inasmuch as you did
it to one of the least of these My brethren,
you did it to Me.'"

MATTHEW 25:40 NKJV

Even so faith, if it hath not works,
is dead, being alone.

JAMES 2:17 KJV

Spiritual Growth

I remind you to fan into flames
the spiritual gift God gave you.
II TIMOTHY 1:6 NLT

As a Christian, you should never stop growing. No matter your age, no matter your circumstances, you have opportunities to learn and opportunities to serve. Wherever you happen to be, God is there, too, and He wants to bless you with an expanding array of spiritual gifts. Your job is to let Him.

The path to spiritual maturity unfolds day by day. Through prayer, through Bible study, and through obedience to God's Word, we can strengthen our relationship with Him. The more we focus on the Father, the more He blesses our lives.

In the quiet moments when we open our hearts to the Lord, the Creator who made us keeps remaking us. He gives us guidance, perspective, courage, and strength. And the appropriate moment to accept these spiritual gifts is always the present one.

Spiritual growth doesn't happen automatically and is rarely pretty; we will all be "under construction" until the day we die and we finally take hold of the "life that is truly life."

KAY WARREN

GOD'S PROMISES ABOUT SPIRITUAL GROWTH

Let perseverance finish its work so that you may be mature and complete, not lacking anything.

JAMES 1:4 NIV

But grow in the grace and knowledge of our Lord and Savior Jesus Christ. To Him be the glory both now and forever. Amen.

II PETER 3:18 NKJV

And be not conformed to this world: but be ye transformed by the renewing of your mind, that ye may prove what is that good, and acceptable, and perfect, will of God.

ROMANS 12:2 KJV

Leave inexperience behind, and you will live; pursue the way of understanding.

PROVERBS 9:6 CSB

So let us stop going over the basic teachings about Christ again and again. Let us go on instead and become mature in our understanding.

HEBREWS 6:1 NLT

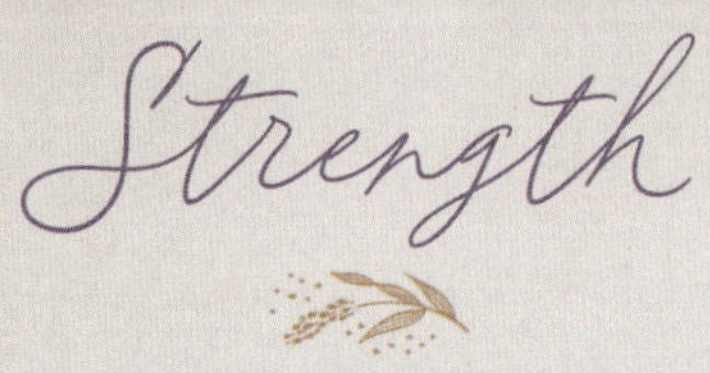

Strength

He gives strength to the weary,
and to him who lacks might He increases power.
ISAIAH 40:29 NASB1995

When you're weary or worried, where do you turn for strength? The medicine cabinet? The gym? The health food store? The spa? These places may offer a temporary energy boost, but the best place to turn for strength and solace isn't down the hall or at the mall; it's as near as your next breath. The best source of strength is God.

God's love for you never changes, and neither does His support. From the cradle to the grave, He has promised to give you the strength to meet the challenges of life. He has promised to guide you and protect you if you let Him. But He also expects you to do your part.

Today provides yet another opportunity to partake in the strength that only God can provide. You do so by attuning your heart to Him through prayer, obedience, and trust. Life can be challenging, but fear not. Whatever your challenge, God can give you the strength to face it and overcome it. Let Him.

Trying to do the Lord's work
in your own strength
is the most confusing, exhausting,
and tedious of all work.
But when you are filled
with the Holy Spirit,
then the ministry of Jesus
just flows out of you.

CORRIE TEN BOOM

GOD'S PROMISES ABOUT STRENGTH

The LORD is my strength and my song;
He has become my salvation.
EXODUS 15:2 CSB

But He said to me,
"My grace is sufficient for you,
for my power is made perfect in weakness."
II CORINTHIANS 12:9 NIV

Have faith in the LORD your God,
and you will stand strong. Have faith in His prophets,
and you will succeed.
II CHRONICLES 20:20 NCV

Be strong and courageous,
and do the work.
Don't be afraid or discouraged,
for the LORD God, my God, is with you.
He won't leave you or abandon you.
I CHRONICLES 28:20 CSB

I can do all things through
Christ who strengthens me.
PHILIPPIANS 4:13 NKJV

Thanksgiving

Enter into His gates with thanksgiving,
and into His courts with praise. Be thankful to Him,
and bless His name. For the LORD is good;
His mercy is everlasting,
and His truth endures to all generations.

PSALM 100:4–5 NKJV

Each of us has much to be thankful for. We all have more blessings than we can count, beginning with the precious gift of life. Every good gift comes from our Father above, and we owe Him our never-ending thanks. But sometimes, when the demands of everyday life press down upon us, we neglect to express our gratitude to the Creator.

God loves us and cares for us; He has a plan for each of us; and He has offered us the gift of eternal life through His Son. Considering all the things that the Lord has done, we owe it to Him—and to ourselves—to slow down many times each day and offer our thanks. His grace is everlasting; our thanks should be too.

Fill up the spare moments of your life with praise and thanksgiving.

SARAH YOUNG

GOD'S PROMISES ABOUT THANKSGIVING

And whatever you do, in word or in deed,
do everything in the name
of the Lord Jesus, giving thanks to God
the Father through Him.

COLOSSIANS 3:17 CSB

*Rejoice always, pray without ceasing,
in everything give thanks; for this is the will of
God in Christ Jesus for you.*

I THESSALONIANS 5:16–18 NKJV

Surely the righteous shall give thanks to Your name;
the upright shall dwell in Your presence.

PSALM 140:13 NKJV

*I will thank the LORD with all my heart;
I will declare all Your wondrous works.
I will rejoice and boast about You;
I will sing about Your name, Most High.*

PSALM 9:1–2 CSB

Thanks be to God for His indescribable gift.

II CORINTHIANS 9:15 CSB

Today

This is the day the Lord has made;
let's rejoice and be glad in it.
PSALM 118:24 CSB

All the days on the calendar have one thing in common: They're all gifts from God. So this day, like every day, is a cause for celebration as we consider God's blessings and His love.

How will you invest this day? Will you treat your time as a commodity too precious to be squandered? Will you carve out time during the day to serve God by serving His children? Will you celebrate God's gifts and obey His commandments? And will you share words of encouragement with the people who cross your path? The answers to these questions will determine, to a surprising extent, the quality of your day and the quality of your life.

So, wherever you find yourself today, take time to celebrate and give thanks for another priceless gift from the Father. The present moment is precious. Treat it that way.

Each day is precious when we consider what we can do to serve God and His kingdom.
ELIZABETH GEORGE

GOD'S PROMISES ABOUT TODAY

But encourage each other
every day while it is "today."
Help each other so none of you
will become hardened
because sin has tricked you.

HEBREWS 3:13 NCV

*"So don't worry about tomorrow,
because tomorrow will have its own worries.
Each day has enough trouble of its own."*

MATTHEW 6:34 NCV

There is a time for everything,
and a season for every
activity under the heavens.

ECCLESIASTES 3:1 NIV

*The world and its desires pass away, but
whoever does the will of God lives forever.*

I JOHN 2:17 NIV

So teach us to number our days,
that we may present to You a heart of wisdom.

PSALM 90:12 NASB

Trusting God

Trust in the LORD with all your heart,
and lean not on your own understanding; in all your ways
acknowledge Him, and He shall direct your paths.

PROVERBS 3:5–6 NKJV

Everywhere we turn, or so it seems, people are asking us to trust them. Advertisers and politicians, businesses and governments all proclaim their trustworthiness. And, of course, many of them are trustworthy. But many of them are not. Oftentimes we are overpromised and underserved. Why? Because mankind is fallen and flawed.

Where will you place your trust today: In fallible humans or in the infallible Creator of the universe? The answer should be obvious.

Today and every day, trust God's promises. Remember that He is always near and that He watches over you. When you are anxious or weak, call upon Him. God can solve your problems better than you can, so turn them over to Him. Remember that the Lord rules both the mountaintops and the valleys—with infinite wisdom and love—now and forever.

Never be afraid to trust an unknown future to a known God.

CORRIE TEN BOOM

GOD'S PROMISES ABOUT TRUSTING HIM

"In quietness and trust is your strength."

ISAIAH 30:15 NASB

The LORD is my rock,
my fortress, and my deliverer, my God,
my rock where I seek refuge.
My shield, the horn of my salvation,
my stronghold, my refuge, and my Savior.

II SAMUEL 22:2–3 CSB

The fear of mankind is a snare,
but the one who trusts
in the LORD is protected.

PROVERBS 29:25 CSB

Those who trust in the LORD are like Mount Zion. It cannot be shaken; it remains forever.

PSALM 125:1 CSB

Jesus said, "Don't let your hearts be troubled. Trust in God, and trust in Me."

JOHN 14:1 NCV

Wisdom and Understanding

The fear of the LORD is the beginning of knowledge,
but fools despise wisdom and instruction.

PROVERBS 1:7 NKJV

God's Word makes this promise: If we genuinely desire wisdom, and if we're willing to search for it, we will find it. And where should the search begin? The answer, of course, is in God's holy Word.

The search for wisdom should be a lifelong journey, not a destination. We should continue to read, to watch, and to learn new things as long as we live. But it's not enough to learn new things or to memorize the great biblical truths; we must also live by them.

So, what will you learn today? Will you take time to feed your mind and fill your heart? And will you study the guidebook that God has given you? Hopefully so, because His plans and His promises are waiting for you there, inside the covers of a book like no other: His Book. It contains the essential wisdom you'll need to navigate the seas of life and land safely on that distant shore.

As we trust God to give us wisdom for today's decisions, He will lead us a step at a time into what He wants us to be doing in the future.

THEODORE EPP

GOD'S PROMISES ABOUT WISDOM AND UNDERSTANDING

Get wisdom—how much
better it is than gold!
And get understanding—
it is preferable to silver.
PROVERBS 16:16 CSB

*But the wisdom that is from above
is first pure, then peaceable, gentle, willing to
yield, full of mercy and good fruits, without
partiality and without hypocrisy.*
JAMES 3:17 NKJV

But if any of you lacks wisdom, let him ask of God,
who gives to all generously and without reproach,
and it will be given to him.
JAMES 1:5 NASB

*Who among you
is wise and understanding?
Let him show by his good behavior
his deeds in the gentleness of wisdom.*
JAMES 3:13 NASB

Work and Dedication

Whatever you do, do it from the heart,
as something done for the Lord and not for people.
COLOSSIANS 3:23 CSB

Time and again, the Bible extols the value of hard work. In Proverbs, we are instructed to take a lesson from a surprising source: ants. Ants are among nature's most industrious creatures. They do their work without supervision, hesitation, or complaint. We should do likewise, but oftentimes we don't. We're tempted to look for shortcuts (there aren't any), or we rely on luck (it happens, but we shouldn't depend on it). Meanwhile, the clock continues to tick, life continues to pass, and important work goes undone.

The book of Proverbs proclaims, "One who is slack in his work is brother to one who destroys" (18:9 NIV). And in his second letter to the Thessalonians, Paul writes, "If any would not work, neither should he eat" (3:10 KJV). In short, God has created a world in which labor is rewarded but laziness is not.

As you think about your own work, please remember that God has big plans for you, and He's given you everything you need to fulfill His purpose. But He won't force His plans upon you, and He won't do all the work. He expects you to do your part. When you do, you'll earn the rewards He most certainly has in store.

All work, if offered to Him,

is transformed.

It is not secular

but sacred,

sanctified in the glad offering.

ELISABETH ELLIOT

GOD'S PROMISES ABOUT WORK AND DEDICATION

But this I say: He who sows sparingly
will also reap sparingly, and he who
sows bountifully will also reap bountifully.

II CORINTHIANS 9:6 NKJV

Be strong and courageous, and do the work.
Don't be afraid or discouraged,
for the LORD God, my God, is with you.
He won't leave you or abandon you.

I CHRONICLES 28:20 CSB

The plans of hard-working people
earn a profit, but those who act
too quickly become poor.

PROVERBS 21:5 NCV

Do you see a man skilled in his work?
He will stand in the presence of kings.

PROVERBS 22:29 CSB

I was glad when they said unto me,
Let us go into the house of the LORD.
PSALM 122:1 KJV

Wise women understand the importance of worship. To worship God is a privilege, but it's a privilege that far too many of us forego. Instead of praising our Creator seven days a week, we worship on Sunday mornings (if at all) and spend the rest of the week focusing on other things.

Whenever we become distracted by worldly pursuits that put God in second place, we inevitably pay the price of our misplaced priorities. A better strategy, of course, is to worship Him every day of the week, beginning with a regular early-morning devotional.

Every new day provides another opportunity to worship God with grateful hearts and helping hands. And each day offers another chance to support the church He created. When we do so, we bless others—and we are blessed by the One who sent His only begotten Son so that we might have eternal life.

Even the most routine part of your day can be a spiritual act of worship.

SARAH YOUNG

GOD'S PROMISES ABOUT WORSHIP

Happy are those who hear
the joyful call to worship,
for they will walk in the light
of your presence, LORD.

PSALM 89:15 NLT

*The whole earth will
worship You and sing praise to You.
They will sing praise to Your name.*

PSALM 66:4 CSB

"God is spirit, and those who worship Him
must worship in Spirit and truth."

JOHN 4:24 CSB

*"For where two or three are gathered together
in My name, I am there among them."*

MATTHEW 18:20 CSB

Worship the LORD with gladness.
Come before Him, singing with joy.
Acknowledge that the LORD is God!
He made us, and we are His.
We are His people, the sheep of His pasture.

PSALM 100:2–3 NLT

Dear Friend,

This book was prayerfully crafted with you, the reader, in mind. Every word, every sentence, every page was thoughtfully written, designed, and packaged to encourage you—right where you are this very moment. At DaySpring, our vision is to see every person experience the life-changing message of God's love. So, as we worked through rough drafts, design changes, edits, and details, we prayed for you to deeply experience His unfailing love, indescribable peace, and pure joy. It is our sincere hope that through these Truth-filled pages your heart will be blessed, knowing that God cares about you—your desires and disappointments, your challenges and dreams.

He knows. He cares. He loves you unconditionally.

BLESSINGS!
THE DAYSPRING BOOK TEAM